MATLAB Control Systems Engineering

César Pérez López

Apress®

MATLAB Control Systems Engineering

ISBN-13 (pbk): 978-1-4842-0290-6

ISBN-13 (electronic): 978-1-4842-0289-0

Publisher: Heinz Weinheimer
Lead Editor: Dominic Shakeshaft
Editorial Board: Steve Anglin, Mark Beckner, Ewan Buckingham, Gary Cornell, Louise Corrigan, Jim DeWolf, Jonathan Gennick, Jonathan Hassell, Robert Hutchinson, Michelle Lowman, James Markham, Matthew Moodie, Jeff Olson, Jeffrey Pepper, Douglas Pundick, Ben Renow-Clarke, Dominic Shakeshaft, Gwenan Spearing, Matt Wade, Steve Weiss
Coordinating Editor: Melissa Maldonado
Copy Editor: Barnaby Sheppard
Compositor: SPi Global
Indexer: SPi Global
Artist: SPi Global
Cover Designer: Anna Ishchenko

Distributed to the book trade worldwide by Springer Science+Business Media New York, 233 Spring Street, 6th Floor, New York, NY 10013. Phone 1-800-SPRINGER, fax (201) 348-4505, e-mail orders-ny@springer-sbm.com, or visit www.springeronline.com. Apress Media, LLC is a California LLC and the sole member (owner) is Springer Science + Business Media Finance Inc (SSBM Finance Inc). SSBM Finance Inc is a Delaware corporation.

For information on translations, please e-mail rights@apress.com, or visit www.apress.com.

Apress and friends of ED books may be purchased in bulk for academic, corporate, or promotional use. eBook versions and licenses are also available for most titles. For more information, reference our Special Bulk Sales-eBook Licensing web page at www.apress.com/bulk-sales.

Any source code or other supplementary material referenced by the author in this text is available to readers at www.apress.com. For detailed information about how to locate your book's source code, go to www.apress.com/source-code/.

Contents at a Glance

Contents

About the Author

César Pérez López is a Professor at the Department of Statistics and Operations Research at the University of Madrid. César is also a Mathematician and Economist at the National Statistics Institute (INE) in Madrid, a body which belongs to the Superior Systems and Information Technology Department of the Spanish Government. César also currently works at the Institute for Fiscal Studies in Madrid.

Coming Soon

- *MATLAB Programming for Numerical Analysis,* 978-1-4842-0296-8
- *MATLAB Differential Equations,* 978-1-4842-0311-8
- *MATLAB Linear Algebra,* 978-1-4842-0323-1
- *MATLAB Differential and Integral Calculus,* 978-1-4842-0305-7
- *MATLAB Matrix Algebra,* 978-1-4842-0308-8

CHAPTER 1

■ ■ ■

Introducing MATLAB and the MATLAB Working Environment

Introduction

MATLAB is a platform for scientific calculation and high-level programming which uses an interactive environment that allows you to conduct complex calculation tasks more efficiently than with traditional languages, such as C, C++ and FORTRAN. It is the one of the most popular platforms currently used in the sciences and engineering.

MATLAB is an interactive high-level technical computing environment for algorithm development, data visualization, data analysis and numerical analysis. MATLAB is suitable for solving problems involving technical calculations using optimized algorithms that are incorporated into easy to use commands.

It is possible to use MATLAB for a wide range of applications, including calculus, algebra, statistics, econometrics, quality control, time series, signal and image processing, communications, control system design, testing and measuring systems, financial modeling, computational biology, etc. The complementary toolsets, called *toolboxes* (collections of MATLAB functions for special purposes, which are available separately), extend the MATLAB environment, allowing you to solve special problems in different areas of application.

In addition, MATLAB contains a number of functions which allow you to document and share your work. It is possible to integrate MATLAB code with other languages and applications, and to distribute algorithms and applications that are developed using MATLAB.

The following are the most important features of MATLAB:

- It is a high-level language for technical calculation

- It offers a development environment for managing code, files and data

- It features interactive tools for exploration, design and iterative solving

- It supports mathematical functions for linear algebra, statistics, Fourier analysis, filtering, optimization, and numerical integration

- It can produce high quality two-dimensional and three-dimensional graphics to aid data visualization

- It includes tools to create custom graphical user interfaces

- It can be integrated with external languages, such as C/C++, FORTRAN, Java, COM, and Microsoft Excel

The MATLAB development environment allows you to develop algorithms, analyze data, display data files and manage projects in interactive mode (see Figure 1-1).

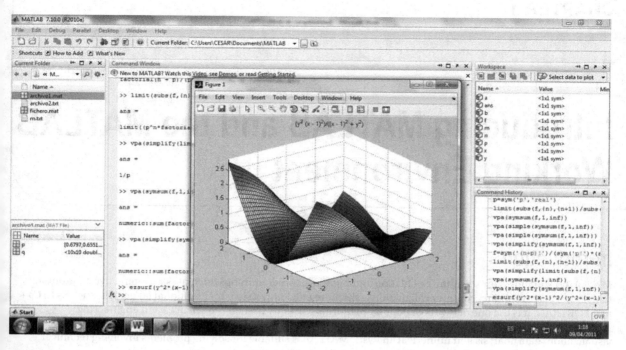

Figure 1-1.

Developing Algorithms and Applications

MATLAB provides a high-level programming language and development tools which enable you to quickly develop and analyze algorithms and applications.

The MATLAB language includes vector and matrix operations that are fundamental to solving scientific and engineering problems. This streamlines both development and execution.

With the MATLAB language, it is possible to program and develop algorithms faster than with traditional languages because it is no longer necessary to perform low-level administrative tasks, such as declaring variables, specifying data types and allocating memory. In many cases, MATLAB eliminates the need for 'for' loops. As a result, a line of MATLAB code usually replaces several lines of C or C++ code.

At the same time, MATLAB offers all the features of traditional programming languages, including arithmetic operators, control flow, data structures, data types, object-oriented programming (OOP) and debugging.

Figure 1-2 shows a communication modulation algorithm that generates 1024 random bits, performs the modulation, adds complex Gaussian noise and graphically represents the result, all in just nine lines of MATLAB code.

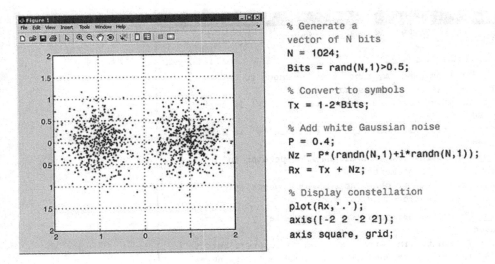

```
% Generate a
vector of N bits
N = 1024;
Bits = rand(N,1)>0.5;

% Convert to symbols
Tx = 1-2*Bits;

% Add white Gaussian noise
P = 0.4;
Nz = P*(randn(N,1)+i*randn(N,1));
Rx = Tx + Nz;

% Display constellation
plot(Rx,'.');
axis([-2 2 -2 2]);
axis square, grid;
```

Figure 1-2.

MATLAB enables you to execute commands or groups of commands one at a time, without compiling or linking, and to repeat the execution to achieve the optimal solution.

To quickly execute complex vector and matrix calculations, MATLAB uses libraries optimized for the processor. For general scalar calculations, MATLAB generates instructions in machine code using JIT (*Just-In-Time*) technology. Thanks to this technology, which is available for most platforms, the execution speeds are much faster than for traditional programming languages.

MATLAB includes *development tools*, which help efficiently implement algorithms. Some of these tools are listed below:

- **MATLAB Editor** – used for editing functions and standard debugging, for example setting breakpoints and running step-by-step simulations

- **M-Lint Code Checker** - analyzes the code and recommends changes to improve performance and maintenance (see Figure 1-3)

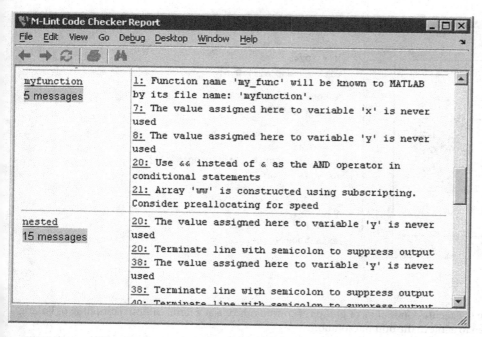

Figure 1-3.

- **MATLAB Profiler** - records the time taken to execute each line of code
- **Directory Reports** - scans all files in a directory and creates reports about the efficiency of the code, differences between files, dependencies of files and code coverage

You can also use the interactive tool GUIDE (*Graphical User Interface Development Environment*) to design and edit user interfaces. This tool allows you to include pick lists, drop-down menus, push buttons, radio buttons and sliders, as well as MATLAB diagrams and ActiveX controls. You can also create graphical user interfaces by means of programming using MATLAB functions.

Figure 1-4 shows a completed wavelet analysis tool (bottom) which has been created using the user interface GUIDE (top).

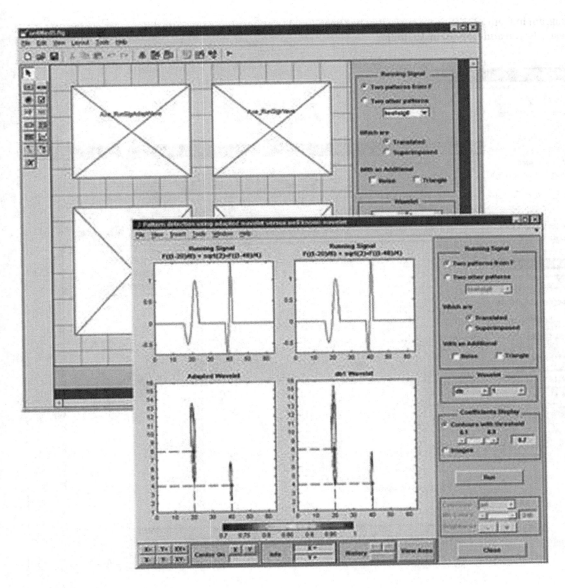

Figure 1-4.

Data Access and Analysis

MATLAB supports the entire process of data analysis, from the acquisition of data from external devices and databases, pre-processing, visualization and numerical analysis, up to the production of results in presentation quality.

MATLAB provides interactive tools and command line operations for data analysis, which include: sections of data, scaling and averaging, interpolation, thresholding and smoothing, correlation, Fourier analysis and filtering, searching for one-dimensional peaks and zeros, basic statistics and curve fitting, matrix analysis, etc.

The diagram in Figure 1-5 shows a curve that has been fitted to atmospheric pressure differences averaged between Easter Island and Darwin in Australia.

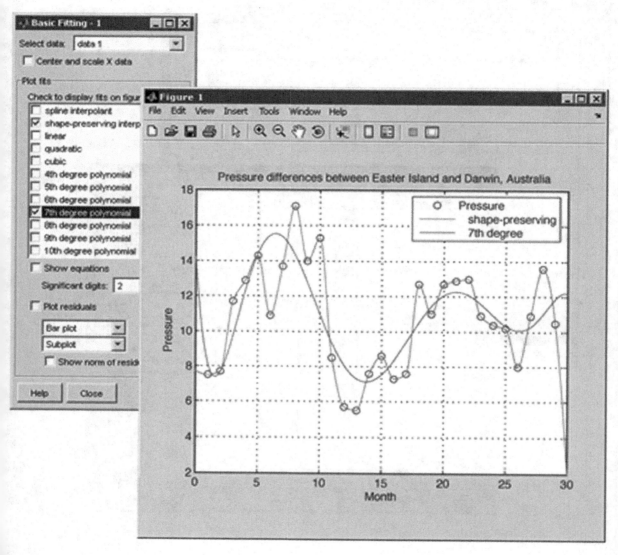

Figure 1-5.

The MATLAB platform allows efficient access to data files, other applications, databases and external devices. You can read data stored in most known formats, such as Microsoft Excel, ASCII text files or binary image, sound and video files, and scientific archives such as HDF and HDF5 files. The binary files for low level I/O functions allow you to work with data files in any format. Additional features allow you to view Web pages and XML data.

It is possible to call other applications and languages, such as C, C++, COM, DLLs, Java, FORTRAN, and Microsoft Excel objects, and access FTP sites and Web services. Using the Database Toolbox, you can even access ODBC/JDBC databases.

Data Visualization

All graphics functions necessary to visualize scientific and engineering data are available in MATLAB. This includes tools for two- and three-dimensional diagrams, three-dimensional volume visualization, tools to create diagrams interactively, and the ability to export using the most popular graphic formats. It is possible to customize diagrams, adding multiple axes, changing the colors of lines and markers, adding annotations, LaTeX equations and legends, and plotting paths.

Various two-dimensional graphical representations of vector data can be created, including:

- Line, area, bar and sector diagrams
- Direction and velocity diagrams
- Histograms
- Polygons and surfaces
- Dispersion bubble diagrams
- Animations

Figure 1-6 shows linear plots of the results of several emission tests of a motor, with a curve fitted to the data.

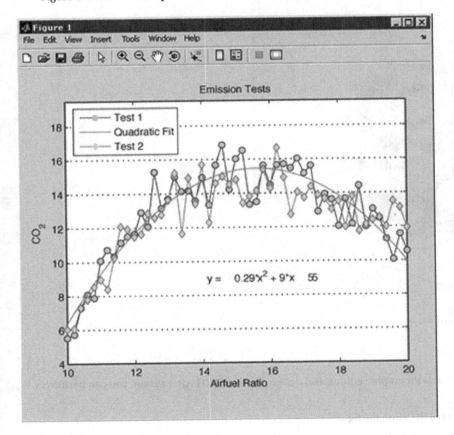

Figure 1-6.

MATLAB also provides functions for displaying two-dimensional arrays, three-dimensional scalar data and three-dimensional vector data. It is possible to use these functions to visualize and understand large amounts of complex multi-dimensional data. It is also possible to define the characteristics of the diagrams, such as the orientation of the camera, perspective, lighting, light source and transparency. Three-dimensional diagramming features include:

- Surface, contour and mesh plots
- Space curves
- Cone, phase, flow and isosurface diagrams

Figure 1-7 shows a three-dimensional diagram of an isosurface that reveals the geodesic structure of a fullerene carbon-60 molecule.

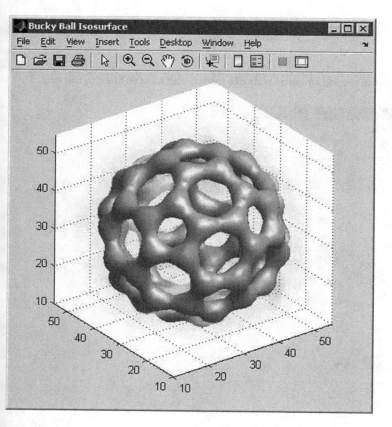

Figure 1-7.

MATLAB includes interactive tools for graphic editing and design. From a MATLAB diagram, you can perform any of the following tasks:

- Drag and drop new sets of data into the figure
- Change the properties of any object in the figure
- Change the zoom, rotation, view (i.e. panoramic), camera angle and lighting

- Add data labels and annotations

- Draw shapes

- Generate an M-file for reuse with different data

Figure 1-8 shows a collection of graphics which have been created interactively by dragging data sets onto the diagram window, making new subdiagrams, changing properties such as colors and fonts, and adding annotations.

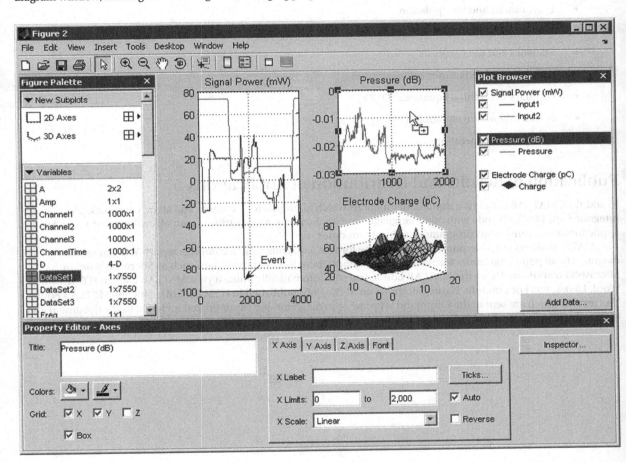

Figure 1-8.

MATLAB is compatible with all the well-known data file and graphics formats, such as GIF, JPEG, BMP, EPS, TIFF, PNG, HDF, AVI, and PCX. As a result, it is possible to export MATLAB diagrams to other applications, such as Microsoft Word and Microsoft PowerPoint, or desktop publishing software. Before exporting, you can create and apply style templates that contain all the design details, fonts, line thickness, etc., necessary to comply with the publication specifications.

Numerical Calculation

MATLAB contains mathematical, statistical, and engineering functions that support most of the operations carried out in those fields. These functions, developed by math experts, are the foundation of the MATLAB language. To cite some examples, MATLAB implements mathematical functions and data analysis in the following areas:

- Manipulation of matrices and linear algebra

- Polynomials and interpolation

- Fourier analysis and filters

- Statistics and data analysis

- Optimization and numerical integration

- Ordinary differential equations (ODEs)

- Partial differential equations (PDEs)

- Sparse matrix operations

Publication of Results and Distribution of Applications

In addition, MATLAB contains a number of functions which allow you to document and share your work. You can integrate your MATLAB code with other languages and applications, and distribute your algorithms and MATLAB applications as autonomous programs or software modules.

MATLAB allows you to export the results in the form of a diagram or as a complete report. You can export diagrams to all popular graphics formats and then import them into other packages such as Microsoft Word or Microsoft PowerPoint. Using the MATLAB Editor, you can automatically publish your MATLAB code in HTML format, Word, LaTeX, etc. For example, Figure 1-9 shows an M-file (left) published in HTML (right) using the MATLAB Editor. The results, which are sent to the Command Window or to diagrams, are captured and included in the document and the comments become titles and text in HTML.

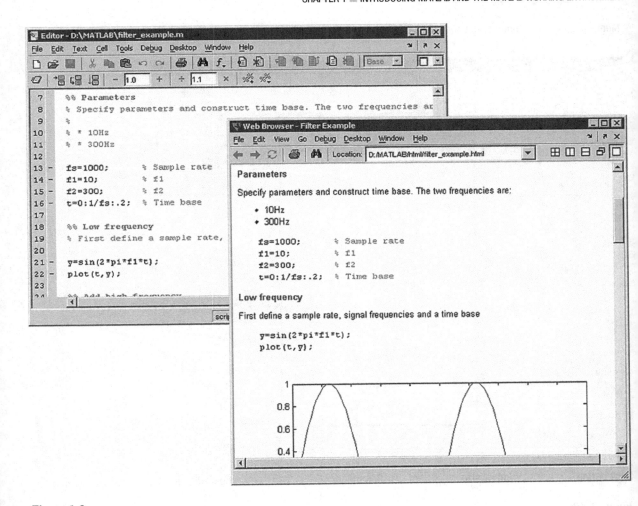

Figure 1-9.

It is possible to create more complex reports, such as mock executions and various parameter tests, using MATLAB Report Generator (available separately).

MATLAB provides functions enabling you to integrate your MATLAB applications with C and C++ code, FORTRAN code, COM objects, and Java code. You can call DLLs and Java classes and ActiveX controls. Using the MATLAB engine library, you can also call MATLAB from C, C++, or FORTRAN code.

You can create algorithms in MATLAB and distribute them to other users of MATLAB. Using the MATLAB Compiler (available separately), algorithms can be distributed, either as standalone applications or as software modules included in a project, to users who do not have MATLAB. Additional products are able to turn algorithms into a software module that can be called from COM or Microsoft Excel.

The MATLAB Working Environment

Figure 1-10 shows the primary workspace of the MATLAB environment. This is the screen in which you enter your MATLAB programs.

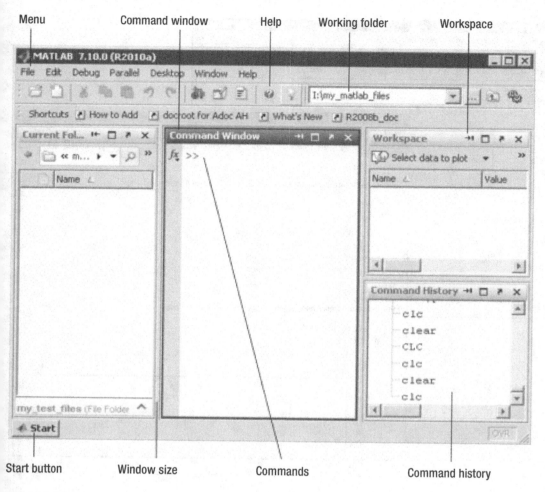

Menu · Command window · Help · Working folder · Workspace

Start button · Window size · Commands · Command history

Figure 1-10.

The following table summarizes the components of the MATLAB environment.

Tool	Description
Command History	This allows you to see the commands entered during the session in the Command Window, as well as copy them and run them (lower right part of Figure 1-11)
Command Window	This is where you enter MATLAB commands (central part of Figure 1-11)
Workspace	This allows you to view the contents of the workspace (variables, etc.) (upper right part of Figure 1-11)
Help	This offers help and demos on MATLAB
Start button	This enables you to run tools and provides access to MATLAB documentation (Figure 1-12)

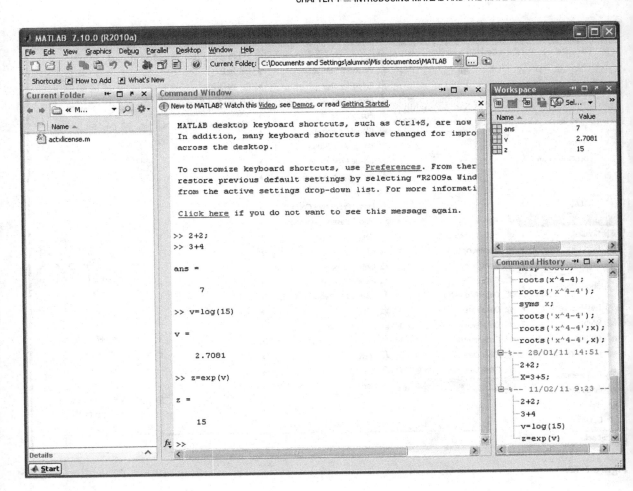

Figure 1-11.

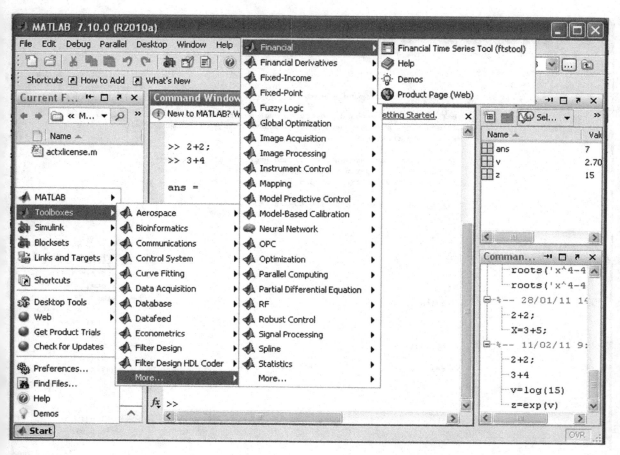

Figure 1-12.

MATLAB commands are written in the Command Window to the right of the user input prompt "»" and the response to the command will appear in the lines immediately below. After exiting from the response, the user input prompt will re-display, allowing you to input more entries (Figure 1-13).

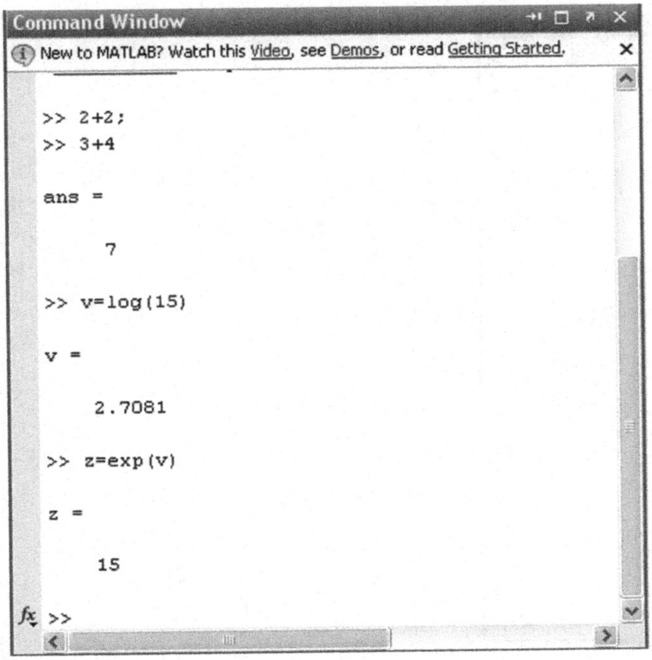

```
Command Window                              →| □  ⤢  ✕
① New to MATLAB? Watch this Video, see Demos, or read Getting Started.    ✕

>> 2+2;
>> 3+4

ans =

     7

>> v=log(15)

v =

    2.7081

>> z=exp(v)

z =

    15

fx >>
```

Figure 1-13.

When an input is given to MATLAB in the Command Window and the result is not assigned to a variable, the response returned will begin with the expression *"**ans=**"*, as shown near the top of Figure 1-13. If the results are assigned to a variable, we can then use that variable as an argument for subsequent input. This is the case for the variable v in Figure 1-13, which is subsequently used as the input for an exponential.

To run a MATLAB command, simply type the command and press *Enter*. If at the end of the input we put a semicolon, the program runs the calculation and keeps it in memory (*Workspace*), but does not display the result on the screen (see the first entry in Figure 1-13). The input prompt "»" appears to indicate that you can enter a new command.

Like the C programming language, MATLAB is case sensitive; for example, $Sin(x)$ is not the same as $sin(x)$. The names of all built-in functions begin with a lowercase character. There should be no spaces in the names of commands, variables or functions. In other cases, spaces are ignored, and they can be used to make the input more readable. Multiple entries can be entered in the same command line by separating them with commas, pressing *Enter* at the end of the last entry (see Figure 1-14). If you use a semicolon at the end of one of the entries in the line, its corresponding output will not be displayed.

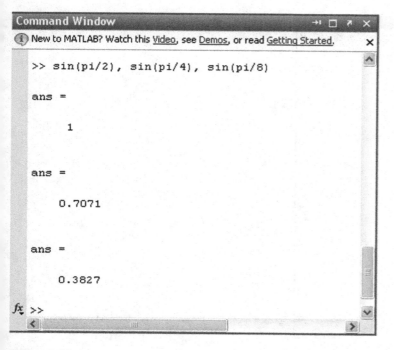

Figure 1-14.

Descriptive comments can be entered in a command input line by starting them with the "%" symbol. When you run the input, MATLAB ignores the comment and processes the rest of the code (see Figure 1-15).

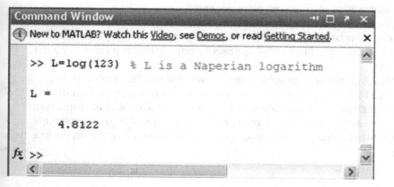

Figure 1-15.

To simplify the process of entering script to be evaluated by the MATLAB interpreter (via the Command Window prompt), you can use the arrow keys. For example, if you press the up arrow key once, you will recover the last entry you submitted. If you press the up key twice, you will recover the penultimate entry you submitted, and so on.

If you type a sequence of characters in the input area and then press the up arrow key, you will recover the last entry you submitted that begins with the specified string.

Commands entered during a MATLAB session are temporarily stored in the buffer (*Workspace*) until you end the session, at which time they can be stored in a file or are permanently lost.

Below is a summary of the keys that can be used in MATLAB's input area (command line), together with their functions:

Up arrow (Ctrl-P)	Retrieves the previous entry.
Down arrow (Ctrl-N)	Retrieves the following entry.
Left arrow (Ctrl-B)	Moves the cursor one character to the left.
Right arrow (Ctrl-F)	Moves the cursor one character to the right.
CTRL-left arrow	Moves the cursor one word to the left.
CTRL-right arrow	Moves the cursor one word to the right.
Home (Ctrl-A)	Moves the cursor to the beginning of the line.
End (Ctrl-E)	Moves the cursor to the end of the current line.
Escape	Clears the command line.
Delete (Ctrl-D)	Deletes the character indicated by the cursor.
Backspace	Deletes the character to the left of the cursor.
CTRL-K	Deletes (kills) the current line.

The command *clc* clears the command window, but does not delete the contents of the work area (the contents remain in the memory).

Help in MATLAB

You can find help for MATLAB via the help button ❷ in the toolbar or via the *Help* option in the menu bar. In addition, support can also be obtained via MATLAB commands. The command *help* provides general help on all MATLAB commands (see Figure 1-16). By clicking on any of them, you can get more specific help. For example, if you click on *graph2d*, you get support for two-dimensional graphics (see Figure 1-17).

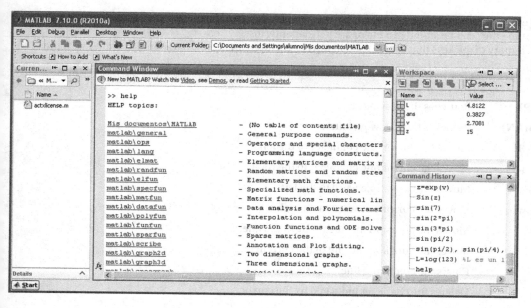

Figure 1-16.

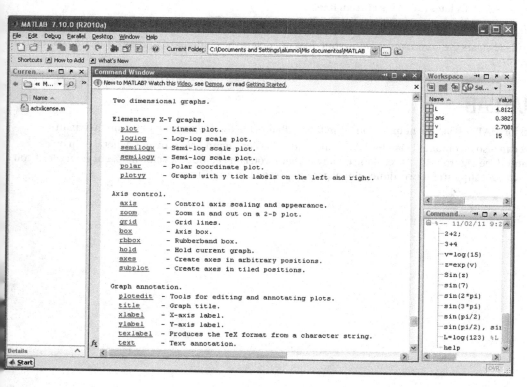

Figure 1-17.

You can ask for help about a specific command *command* (Figure 1-18) or on any topic *topic* (Figure 1-19) by using the command *help command* or *help topic*.

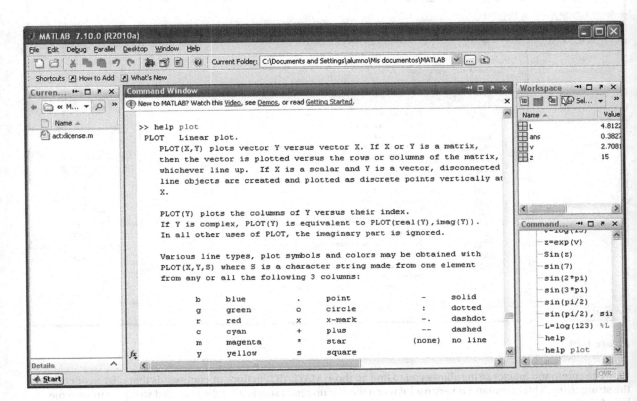

Figure 1-18.

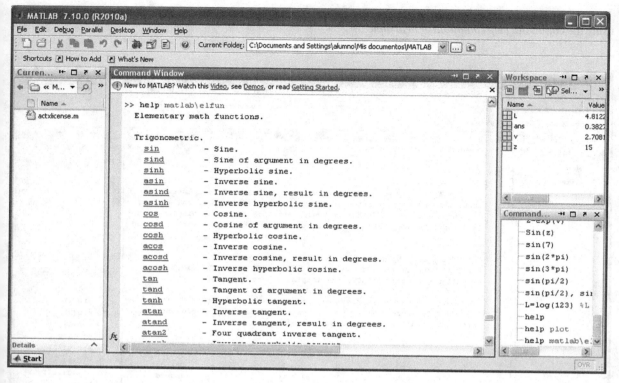

Figure 1-19.

The command *lookfor string* allows you to find all those MATLAB functions or commands that refer to or contain the string *string*. This command is very useful when there is no direct support for the specified string, or to view the help for all commands related to the given string. For example, if we want to find help for all commands that contain the sequence *inv*, we can use the command *lookfor inv* (Figure 1-20).

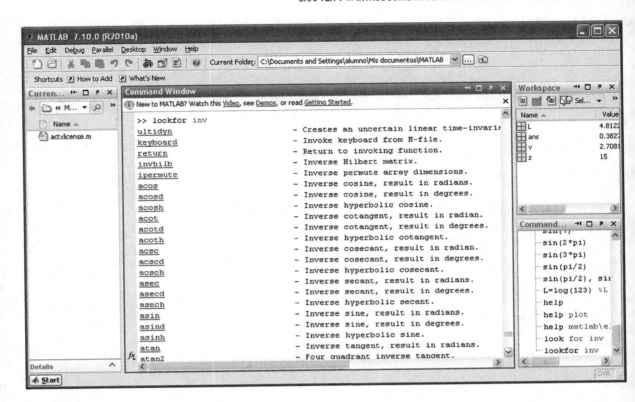

Figure 1-20.

CHAPTER 2

■ ■ ■

Variables, Numbers, Operators and Functions

Variables

MATLAB does not require a command to declare variables. A variable is created simply by directly allocating a value to it. For example:

```
>> v = 3

v =

3
```

The variable v will take the value 3 and using a new mapping will not change its value. Once the variable is declared, we can use it in calculations.

```
>> v ^ 3

ans =

27

>> v + 5

ans =

8
```

The value assigned to a variable remains fixed until it is explicitly changed or if the current MATLAB session is closed.

If we now write:

```
>> v = 3 + 7

v =

10
```

then the variable v has the value 10 from now on, as shown in the following calculation:

```
>> v ^ 4
```

ans =

10000

A variable name must begin with a letter followed by any number of letters, digits or underscores. However, bear in mind that MATLAB uses only the first 31 characters of the name of the variable. It is also very important to note that MATLAB is case sensitive. Therefore, a variable named with uppercase letters is different to the variable with the same name except in lowercase letters.

Vector Variables

A vector variable of n elements can be defined in MATLAB in the following ways:

```
V = [v1, v2, v3,..., vn]
```

```
V = [v1 v2 v3... vn]
```

When most MATLAB commands and functions are applied to a vector variable the result is understood to be that obtained by applying the command or function to each element of the vector:

```
>> vector1 = [1,4,9,2.25,1/4]
```

vector1 =

1.0000 4.0000 9.0000 2.2500 0.2500

```
>> sqrt (vector1)
```

ans =

1.0000 2.0000 3.0000 1.5000 0.5000

The following table presents some alternative ways of defining a vector variable without explicitly bracketing all its elements together, separated by commas or blank spaces.

variable = [a:b]	*Defines the vector whose first and last elements are a and b, respectively, and the intermediate elements differ by one unit.*
variable = [a:s:b]	*Defines the vector whose first and last elements are a and b, respectively, and the intermediate elements differ by an increase specified by s.*
variable = linespace [a, b, n]	*Defines the vector with n evenly spaced elements whose first and last elements are a and b respectively.*
variable = logspace [a, b, n]	*Defines the vector with n evenly logarithmically spaced elements whose first and last elements are 10^a and 10^b, respectively.*

Below are some examples:

```
>> vector2 = [5:5:25]
```

vector2 =

5 10 15 20 25

This yields the numbers between 5 and 25, inclusive, separated by 5 units.

```
>> vector3=[10:30]
```

vector3 =

Columns 1 through 13

10   11   12   13   14   15   16   17   18   19   20   21   22

Columns 14 through 21

23 24 25 26 27 28 29 30

This yields the numbers between 10 and 30, inclusive, separated by a unit.

```
>> t:Microsoft.WindowsMobile.DirectX.Vector4 = linspace (10,30,6)
```

t:Microsoft.WindowsMobile.DirectX.Vector4 =

10 14 18 22 26 30

This yields 6 equally spaced numbers between 10 and 30, inclusive.

```
>> vector5 = logspace (10,30,6)
```

vector5 =

*1. 0e + 030 **

0.0000 0.0000 0.0000 0.0000 0.0001 1.0000

This yields 6 evenly logarithmically spaced numbers between 10^{10} and 10^{30}, inclusive.

One can also consider row vectors and column vectors in MATLAB. A column vector is obtained by separating its elements by semicolons, or by transposing a row vector using a single quotation mark at the end of its definition.

```
>> a = [10;20;30;40]
```

a =

10
20
30
40

```
>> a = (10:14);b = a'
```

b =

10
11
12
13
14

```
>> c = (a')'
```

c =

10 11 12 13 14

You can also select an element of a vector or a subset of elements. The rules are summarized in the following table:

x (n)	*Returns the n-th element of the vector x.*
x(a:b)	*Returns the elements of the vector x between the a-th and the b-th elements, inclusive.*
x(a:p:b)	*Returns the elements of the vector x located between the a-th and the b-th elements, inclusive, but separated by p units (a > b).*
x(b:-p:a)	*Returns the elements of the vector x located between the b-th and a-th elements, both inclusive, but separated by p units and starting with the b-th element (b > a).*

Here are some examples:

```
>> x = (1:10)
```

x =

1   2   3   4   5   6   7   8   9   10

```
>> x (6)
```

ans =

6

This yields the sixth element of the vector *x*.

```
>> x (4:7)
```

ans =

4 5 6 7

This yields the elements of the vector x located between the fourth and seventh elements, inclusive.

>> x(2:3:9)

ans =

2 5 8

This yields the three elements of the vector x located between the second and ninth elements, inclusive, but separated in steps of three units.

>> x(9:-3:2)

ans =

9 6 3

This yields the three elements of the vector x located between the ninth and second elements, inclusive, but separated in steps of three units and starting at the ninth.

Matrix Variables

MATLAB defines arrays by inserting in brackets all its row vectors separated by a semicolon. Vectors can be entered by separating their components by spaces or by commas, as we already know. For example, a 3 × 3 matrix variable can be entered in the following two ways:

$$M = [a_{11}\ a_{12}\ a_{13}; a_{21}\ a_{22}\ a_{23}; a_{31}\ a_{32}\ a_{33}]$$
$$M = [a_{11}, a_{12}, a_{13}; a_{21}, a_{22}, a_{23}; a_{31}, a_{32}, a_{33}]$$

Similarly we can define an array of variable dimension $(M \times N)$. Once a matrix variable has been defined, MATLAB enables many ways to insert, extract, renumber, and generally manipulate its elements. The following table shows different ways to define matrix variables.

A(m,n)	*Defines the (m, n)-th element of the matrix A (row m and column n).*
A(a:b,c:d)	*Defines the subarray of A formed between the a-th and the b-th rows and between the c-th and the d-th columns, inclusive.*
A(a:p:b,c:q:d)	*Defines the subarray of A formed by every p-th row between the a-th and the b-th rows, inclusive, and every q-th column between the c-th and the d-th column, inclusive.*
A([a b],[c d])	*Defines the subarray of A formed by the intersection of the a-th through b-th rows and c-th through d-th columns, inclusive.*
A([a b c...],[e f g...])	*Defines the subarray of A formed by the intersection of rows a, b, c,...and columns e, f, g,...*
A(:,c:d)	*Defines the subarray of A formed by all the rows in A and the c-th through to the d-th columns.*
A(:,[c d e...])	*Defines the subarray of A formed by all the rows in A and columns c, d, e,...*
A(a:b,:)	*Defines the subarray of A formed by all the columns in A and the a-th through to the b-th rows.*
A([a b c...],:)	*Defines the subarray of A formed by all the columns in A and rows a, b, c,...*

(continued)

A(a,:)	*Defines the a-th row of the matrix A.*
A(:,b)	*Defines the b-th column of the matrix A.*
A(:)	*Defines a column vector whose elements are the columns of A placed in order below each other.*
A(:,:)	*This is equivalent to the entire matrix A.*
[A, B, C,...]	*Defines the matrix formed by the matrices A, B, C,...*
S_A = [ ]	*Clears the subarray of the matrix A, S_A, and returns the remainder.*
diag (v)	*Creates a diagonal matrix with the vector v in the diagonal.*
diag (A)	*Extracts the diagonal of the matrix as a column vector.*
eye (n)	*Creates the identity matrix of order n.*
eye (m, n)	*Creates an m×n matrix with ones on the main diagonal and zeros elsewhere.*
zeros (m, n)	*Creates the zero matrix of order m×n.*
ones (m, n)	*Creates the matrix of order m×n with all its elements equal to 1.*
rand (m, n)	*Creates a uniform random matrix of order m×n.*
randn (m, n)	*Creates a normal random matrix of order m×n.*
flipud (A)	*Returns the matrix whose rows are those of A but placed in reverse order (from top to bottom).*
fliplr (A)	*Returns the matrix whose columns are those of A but placed in reverse order (from left to right).*
rot90 (A)	*Rotates the matrix A counterclockwise by 90 degrees.*
reshape(A,m,n)	*Returns an m×n matrix formed by taking consecutive entries of A by columns.*
size (A)	*Returns the order (size) of the matrix A.*
find (condA)	*Returns all A items that meet a given condition.*
length (v)	*Returns the length of the vector v.*
tril (A)	*Returns the lower triangular part of the matrix A.*
triu (A)	*Returns the upper triangular part of the matrix A.*
A'	*Returns the transpose of the matrix A.*
Inv (A)	*Returns the inverse of the matrix A.*

Here are some examples:
We consider first the *2 × 3* matrix whose rows are the first six consecutive odd numbers:

```
>> A = [1 3 5; 7 9 11]

A =

1 3 5
7 9 11
```

Now we are going to change the *(2,3)-th* element, i.e. the last element of *A*, to zero:

```
>> A(2,3) = 0
```

A =

```
1 3 5
7 9 0
```

We now define the matrix *B* to be the transpose of *A*:

```
>> B = A'
```

B =

```
1 7
3 9
5 0
```

We now construct a matrix *C*, formed by attaching the identity matrix of order 3 to the right of the matrix *B*:

```
>> C = [B eye (3)]
```

C =

```
1    7    1    0    0
3    9    0    1    0
5    0    0    0    1
```

We are going to build a matrix *D* by extracting the odd columns of the matrix *C*, a matrix *E* formed by taking the intersection of the first two rows of *C* and its third and fifth columns, and a matrix *F* formed by taking the intersection of the first two rows and the last three columns of the matrix *C*:

```
>> D = C(:,1:2:5)
```

D =

```
1 1 0
3 0 0
5 0 1
```

```
>> E = C([1 2],[3 5])
```

E =

```
1 0
0 0
```

```
>> F = C([1 2],3:5)

F =

1 0 0
0 1 0
```

Now we build the diagonal matrix G such that the elements of the main diagonal are the same as those of the main diagonal of D:

```
>> G = diag(diag(D))

G =

1 0 0
0 0 0
0 0 1
```

We then build the matrix *H*, formed by taking the intersection of the first and third rows of *C* and its second, third and fifth columns:

```
>> H = C([1 3],[2 3 5])

H =

7 1 0
0 0 1
```

Now we build an array *I* formed by the identity matrix of order 5 × 4, appending the zero matrix of the same order to its right and to the right of that the unit matrix, again of the same order. Then we extract the first row of *I* and, finally, form the matrix *J* comprising the odd rows and even columns of *I* and calculate its order (size).

```
>> I = [eye(5,4) zeros(5,4) ones(5,4)]

ans =

1   0   0   0   0   0   0   0   1   1   1   1
0   1   0   0   0   0   0   0   1   1   1   1
0   0   1   0   0   0   0   0   1   1   1   1
0   0   0   1   0   0   0   0   1   1   1   1
0   0   0   0   0   0   0   0   1   1   1   1

>> I(1,:)

ans =

1   0   0   0   0   0   0   0   1   1   1   1
```

```
>> J = I(1:2:5,2:2:12)
```

J =

```
0    0    0    0    1    1
0    0    0    0    1    1
0    0    0    0    1    1
```

```
>> size(J)
```

ans =

3 6

We now construct a random matrix *K* of order *3 ×4*, reverse the order of the rows of *K*, reverse the order of the columns of *K* and then perform both operations simultaneously. Finally, we find the matrix *L* of order *4 × 3* whose columns are obtained by taking the elements of *K* sequentially by columns.

```
>> K = rand(3,4)
```

K =

```
0.5269    0.4160    0.7622    0.7361
0.0920    0.7012    0.2625    0.3282
0.6539    0.9103    0.0475    0.6326
```

```
>> K(3:-1:1,:)
```

ans =

```
0.6539    0.9103    0.0475    0.6326
0.0920    0.7012    0.2625    0.3282
0.5269    0.4160    0.7622    0.7361
```

```
>> K(:,4:-1:1)
```

ans =

```
0.7361    0.7622    0.4160    0.5269
0.3282    0.2625    0.7012    0.0920
0.6326    0.0475    0.9103    0.6539
```

```
>> K(3:-1:1,4:-1:1)
```

ans =

```
0.6326    0.0475    0.9103    0.6539
0.3282    0.2625    0.7012    0.0920
0.7361    0.7622    0.4160    0.5269
```

```
>> L = reshape(K,4,3)
```

L =

```
0.5269 0.7012 0.0475
0.0920 0.9103 0.7361
0.6539 0.7622 0.3282
0.4160 0.2625 0.6326
```

Character Variables

A character variable (chain) is simply a character string enclosed in single quotes that MATLAB treats as a vector form. The general syntax for character variables is as follows:

c = 'string'

Among the MATLAB commands that handle character variables we have the following:

abs ('character_string')	*Returns the array of ASCII characters equivalent to each character in the string.*
setstr (numeric_vector)	*Returns the string of ASCII characters that are equivalent to the elements of the vector.*
str2mat (t1,t2,t3,...)	*Returns the matrix whose rows are the strings t1, t2, t3,..., respectively*
str2num ('string')	*Converts the string to its exact numeric value used by MATLAB.*
num2str (number)	*Returns the exact number in its equivalent string with fixed precision.*
int2str (integer)	*Converts the integer to a string.*
sprintf ('format', a)	*Converts a numeric array into a string in the specified format.*
sscanf ('string', 'format')	*Converts a string to a numeric value in the specified format.*
dec2hex (integer)	*Converts a decimal integer into its equivalent string in hexadecimal.*
hex2dec ('string_hex')	*Converts a hexadecimal string into its integer equivalent.*
hex2num ('string_hex')	*Converts a hexadecimal string into the equivalent IEEE floating point number.*
lower ('string')	*Converts a string to lowercase.*
upper ('string')	*Converts a string to uppercase.*
strcmp (s1, s2)	*Compares the strings s1 and s2 and returns 1 if they are equal and 0 otherwise.*
strcmp (s1, s2, n)	*Compares the strings s1 and s2 and returns 1 if their first n characters are equal and 0 otherwise.*
strrep (c, 'exp1', 'exp2')	*Replaces exp1 by exp2 in the chain c.*
findstr (c, 'exp')	*Finds where exp is in the chain c.*
isstr (expression)	*Returns 1 if the expression is a string and 0 otherwise.*
ischar (expression)	*Returns 1 if the expression is a string and 0 otherwise.*
strjust (string)	*Right justifies the string.*
blanks (n)	*Generates a string of n spaces.*

(continued)

deblank (string)	*Removes blank spaces from the right of the string.*
eval (expression)	*Executes the expression, even if it is a string.*
disp ('string')	*Displays the string (or array) as has been written, and continues the MATLAB process.*
input ('string')	*Displays the string on the screen and waits for a key press to continue.*

Here are some examples:

```
>> hex2dec ('3ffe56e')
```

ans =

67102062

Here MATLAB has converted a hexadecimal string into a decimal number.

```
>> dec2hex (1345679001)
```

ans =

50356E99

The program has converted a decimal number into a hexadecimal string.

```
>> sprintf('%f',[1+sqrt(5)/2,pi])
```

ans =

2.118034 3.141593

The exact numerical components of a vector have been converted to strings (with default precision).

```
>> sscanf('121.00012', '%f')
```

ans =

121.0001

Here a numeric string has been passed to an exact numerical format (with default precision).

```
>> num2str (pi)
```

ans =

3.142

The constant π has been converted into a string.

```
>> str2num('15/14')
```

ans =

1.0714

The string has been converted into a numeric value with default precision.

```
>> setstr(32:126)
```

ans =

*!"#$% &' () * +, -. / 0123456789:; < = >? @ABCDEFGHIJKLMNOPQRSTUVWXYZ [\] ^*
_'abcdefghijklmnopqrstuvwxyz {|}~

This yields the ASCII characters associated with the whole numbers between 32 and 126, inclusive.

```
>> abs('{|]}><#¡¿?ºª')
```

ans =

123 93 125 62 60 35 161 191 63 186 170

This yields the integers corresponding to the ASCII characters specified in the argument of *abs*.

```
>> lower ('ABCDefgHIJ')
```

ans =

abcdefghij

The text has been converted to lowercase.

```
>> upper('abcd eFGHi jKlMn')
```

ans =

ABCD EFGHI JKLMN

The text has been converted to uppercase.

```
>> str2mat ('The world',' The country',' Daily 16', ' ABC')
```

ans =

The world
The country
Daily 16
ABC

The chains comprising the arguments of *str2mat* have been converted to a text array.

```
>> disp('This text will appear on the screen')
```

ans =

This text will appear on the screen

Here the argument of the command *disp* has been displayed on the screen.

```
>> c = 'This is a good example';
>> strrep(c, 'good', 'bad')
```

ans =

This is a bad example

The string *good* has been replaced by *bad* in the chain *c*. The following instruction locates the initial position of each occurrence of *is* within the chain *c*.

```
>> findstr (c, 'is')
```

ans =

3 6

Numbers

In MATLAB the arguments of a function can take many different forms, including different types of numbers and numerical expressions, such as integers and rational, real and complex numbers.

Arithmetic operations in MATLAB are defined according to the standard mathematical conventions. MATLAB is an interactive program that allows you to perform a simple variety of mathematical operations. MATLAB assumes the usual operations of sum, difference, product, division and power, with the usual hierarchy between them:

x + y	*Sum*
x y	*Difference*
x * y or x y	*Product*
x/y	*Division*
x ^ y	*Power*

To add two numbers simply enter the first number, a plus sign (+) and the second number. Spaces may be included before and after the sign to ensure that the input is easier to read.

```
>> 2 + 3
```

ans =

5

We can perform power calculations directly.

```
>> 100 ^ 50
```

ans =

1. 0000e + 100

Unlike a calculator, when working with integers, MATLAB displays the full result even when there are more digits than would normally fit across the screen. For example, MATLAB returns the following value of *99 ^ 50* when using the vpa function (here to the default accuracy of 32 significant figures).

```
>> vpa '99 ^ 50'
```

ans =

. 60500606713753665044791996801256e100

To combine several operations in the same instruction one must take into account the usual priority criteria among them, which determine the order of evaluation of the expression. Consider, for example:

```
>> 2 * 3 ^ 2 + (5-2) * 3
```

ans =

27

Taking into account the priority of operators, the first expression to be evaluated is the power 3^2. The usual evaluation order can be altered by grouping expressions together in parentheses.

In addition to these arithmetic operators, MATLAB is equipped with a set of basic functions and you can also define your own functions. MATLAB functions and operators can be applied to symbolic constants or numbers.

One of the basic applications of MATLAB is its use in realizing arithmetic operations as if it were a conventional calculator, but with one important difference: the precision of the calculation. Operations are performed to whatever degree of precision the user desires. This unlimited precision in calculation is a feature which sets MATLAB apart from other numerical calculation programs, where the accuracy is determined by a word length inherent to the software, and cannot be modified.

The accuracy of the output of MATLAB operations can be relaxed using special approximation techniques which are exact only up to a certain specified degree of precision. MATLAB represents results with accuracy, but even if internally you are always working with exact calculations to prevent propagation of rounding errors, different approximate representation formats can be enabled, which sometimes facilitate the interpretation of the results. The commands that allow numerical approximation are the following:

format long	*Delivers results to 16 significant decimal figures.*
format short	*Delivers results to 4 decimal places. This is MATLAB's default format.*
format long e	*Provides the results to 16 decimal figures more than the power of 10 required.*
format short e	*Provides the results to four decimal figures more than the power of 10 required.*
format long g	*Provides the results in optimal long format.*
format short g	*Provides the results in optimum short format.*

(continued)

bank format	*Delivers results to 2 decimal places.*
format rat	*Returns the results in the form of a rational number approximation.*
format +	*Returns the sign (+, -) and ignores the imaginary part of complex numbers.*
format hex	*Returns results in hexadecimal format.*
vpa 'operations' n	*Returns the result of the specified operations to n significant digits.*
numeric ('expr')	*Provides the value of the expression numerically approximated by the current active format.*
digits (n)	*Returns results to n significant digits.*

Using *format* gives a numerical approximation of 174/13 in the way specified after the format command:

```
>> 174/13
```

ans =

13.3846

```
>> format long; 174/13
```

ans =

13.38461538461539

```
>> format long e; 174/13
```

ans =

1.338461538461539e + 001

```
>> format short e; 174/13
```

ans =

1.3385e + 001

```
>> format long g; 174/13
```

ans =

13.3846153846154

```
>> format short g; 174/13
```

ans =

13.385

```
>> format bank; 174/13
```

ans =

13.38

```
>> format hex; 174/13
```

ans =

402ac4ec4ec4ec4f

Now we will see how the value of *sqrt (17)* can be calculated to any precision that we desire:

```
>> vpa ' 174/13 ' 10
```

ans =

13.38461538

```
>> vpa ' 174/13 ' 15
```

ans =

13.3846153846154

```
>> digits (20); vpa ' 174/13 '
```

ans =

13.384615384615384615

Integers

In MATLAB all common operations with whole numbers are exact, regardless of the size of the output. If we want the result of an operation to appear on screen to a certain number of significant figures, we use the symbolic computation command ***vpa*** (*variable precision arithmetic*), whose syntax we already know.

For example, the following calculates 6^400 to 450 significant figures:

```
>> '6 vpa ^ 400' 450
```

ans =

*182179771682187282513946871240893712673389715281747606674596975493339599720905327003028267800766283
86733147959945591636745242157445605964680105495406215017704234999886990788594743994796171248406730 9
7380736524850563115569208508785942830080999927310762507339484047393505519345657439796788241511972 32
629947748581376.*

The result of the operation is precise, always displaying a point at the end of the result. In this case it turns out that the answer has fewer than 450 digits anyway, so the solution is exact. If you require a smaller number of significant figures, that number can be specified and the result will be rounded accordingly. For example, calculating the above power to only 50 significant figures we have:

```
>>  '6 vpa ^ 400' 50
```

ans =

. *18217977168218728251394687124089371267338971528175e312*

Functions of Integers and Divisibility

There are several functions in MATLAB with integer arguments, the majority of which are related to divisibility. Among the most typical functions with integer arguments are the following:

rem (n, m)	*Returns the remainder of the division of n by m (also valid when n and m are real).*
sign (n)	*The sign of n (i.e. 1 if n > 0, - 1 if n < 0).*
max (n1, n2)	*The maximum of n1 and n2.*
min (n1, n2)	*The minimum of n1 and n2.*
gcd (n1, n2)	*The greatest common divisor of n1 and n2.*
lcm (n1, n2)	*The least common multiple of n1 and n2.*
factorial (n)	*n factorial (i.e. n(n-1) (n-2)...1)*
factor (n)	*Returns the prime factorization of n.*

Below are some examples.
The remainder of division of 17 by 3:

```
>> rem (17,3)
```

ans =

2

The remainder of division of 4.1 by 1.2:

```
>> rem (4.1,1.2)
```

ans =

0.5000

The remainder of division of - 4.1 by 1.2:

```
>> rem (-4.1,1.2)
```

ans =

-0.5000

The greatest common divisor of 1000, 500 and 625:

```
>> gcd (1000, gcd (500,625))
```

ans =

125.00

The least common multiple of 1000, 500 and 625:

```
>> lcm (1000, lcm (500,625))
```

ans =

5000.00

Alternative Bases

MATLAB allows you to work with numbers to any base, as long as the extended symbolic math *toolbox* is available. It also allows you to express all kinds of numbers in different bases. This is implemented via the following functions:

dec2base (decimal, n_base)	*Converts the specified decimal number to the new base n_base.*
base2dec(number,b)	*Converts the given number in base b to a decimal number.*
dec2bin (decimal)	*Converts the specified decimal number to base 2 (binary).*
dec2hex (decimal)	*Converts the specified decimal number to base 16 (hexadecimal).*
bin2dec (binary)	*Converts the specified binary number to decimal.*
hex2dec (hexadecimal)	*Converts the specified base 16 number to decimal.*

Below are some examples.
Represent in base 10 the base 2 number 100101.

```
>> base2dec('100101',2)
```

ans =

37.00

Represent in base 10 the hexadecimal number FFFFAA00.

```
>> base2dec ('FFFFAA0', 16)
```

ans =

268434080.00

Represent the result of the base 16 operation FFFAA2+FF-1 in base 10.

```
>> base2dec('FFFAA2',16) + base2dec('FF',16)-1
```

ans =

16776096.00

Real Numbers

As is well known, the set of real numbers is the disjoint union of the set of rational numbers and the set of irrational numbers. A rational number is a number of the form p/q, where p and q are integers. In other words, the rational numbers are those numbers that can be represented as a quotient of two integers. The way in which MATLAB treats rational numbers differs from the majority of calculators. If we ask a calculator to calculate the sum $1/2 + 1/3 + 1/4$, most will return something like *1.0833*, which is no more than an approximation of the result.

The rational numbers are ratios of integers, and MATLAB can work with them in exact mode, so the result of an arithmetic expression involving rational numbers is always given precisely as a ratio of two integers. To enable this, activate the rational format with the command *format rat*. If the reader so wishes, MATLAB can also return the results in decimal form by activating any other type of format instead (e.g. *format short* or *format long*). MATLAB evaluates the above mentioned sum in exact mode as follows:

```
>> format rat
>> 1/2 + 1/3 + 1/4
```

ans =

13/12

Unlike calculators, MATLAB ensures its operations with rational numbers are accurate by maintaining the rational numbers in the form of ratios of integers. In this way, calculations with fractions are not affected by rounding errors, which can become very serious, as evidenced by the theory of errors. Note that, once the rational format is enabled, when MATLAB adds two rational numbers the result is returned in symbolic form as a ratio of integers, and operations with rational numbers will continue to be exact until an alternative format is invoked.

A floating point number, or a number with a decimal point, is interpreted as exact if the rational format is enabled. Thus a floating point expression will be interpreted as an exact rational expression while any irrational numbers in a rational expression will be represented by an appropriate rational approximation.

```
>> format rat
>> 10/23 + 2.45/44
```

ans =

1183 / 2412

The other fundamental subset of the real numbers is the set of irrational numbers, which have always created difficulties in numerical calculation due to their special nature. The impossibility of representing an irrational number accurately in numeric mode (using the ten digits from the decimal numbering system) is the cause of most of the problems. MATLAB represents the results with an accuracy which can be set as required by the user. An irrational number, by definition, cannot be represented exactly as the ratio of two integers. If ordered to calculate the square root of 17, by default MATLAB returns the number 5.1962.

```
>> sqrt (27)
```

ans =

5.1962

MATLAB incorporates the following common irrational constants and notions:

pi	*The number $\pi = 3.1415926...$*
exp (1)	*The number $e = 2.7182818...$*
Inf	*Infinity (returned, for example, when it encounters 1/0).*
NaN	*Uncertainty (returned, for example, when it encounters 0/0).*
realmin	*Returns the smallest possible normalized floating-point number in IEEE double precision.*
realmax	*Returns the largest possible finite floating-point number in IEEE double precision.*

The following examples illustrate how MATLAB outputs these numbers and notions.

```
>> long format
>> pi
```

ans =

3.14159265358979

```
>> exp (1)
```

ans =
2.71828182845905

```
>> 1/0
```

Warning: Divide by zero.

ans =

Inf

```
>> 0/0
```

Warning: Divide by zero.

ans =

NaN

```
>> realmin
```

ans =

2. 225073858507201e-308

```
>> realmax
```

ans =

1. 797693134862316e + 308

Functions with Real Arguments

The disjoint union of the set of rational numbers and the set of irrational numbers is the set of real numbers. In turn, the set of rational numbers has the set of integers as a subset. All functions applicable to real numbers are also valid for integers and rational numbers. MATLAB provides a full range of predefined functions, most of which are discussed in the subsequent chapters of this book. Within the group of functions with real arguments offered by MATLAB, the following are the most important:

Trigonometric functions

Function	Inverse
sin (x)	asin (x)
cos (x)	acos (x)
tan(x)	atan(x) and atan2(y,x)
csc (x)	acsc (x)
sec (x)	asec (x)
cot (x)	acot (x)

Hyperbolic functions

Function	Inverse
sinh (x)	asinh (x)
cosh(x)	acosh(x)
tanh(x)	atanh(x)
csch(x)	acsch(x)
sech(x)	asech(x)
coth (x)	acoth (x)

Exponential and logarithmic functions

Function	Meaning
exp (x)	*Exponential function in base e (e ^ x).*
log (x)	*Base e logarithm of x.*
log10 (x)	*Base 10 logarithm of x.*
log2 (x)	*Base 2 logarithm of x.*
pow2 (x)	*2 raised to the power x.*
sqrt (x)	*The square root of x.*

Numeric variable-specific functions

Function	Meaning
abs (x)	*The absolute value of x.*
floor (x)	*The largest integer less than or equal to x.*
ceil (x)	*The smaller integer greater than or equal to x.*
round (x)	*The closest integer to x.*
fix (x)	*Removes the fractional part of x.*
rem (a, b)	*Returns the remainder of the division of a by b.*
sign (x)	*Returns the sign of x (1 if x > 0,0 if x = 0,- 1 if x < 0).*

Here are some examples:

```
>> sin(pi/2)
```

ans =

1

```
>> asin (1)
```

ans =

1.57079632679490

```
>> log (exp (1) ^ 3)
```

ans =

3.00000000000000

The function *round* is demonstrated in the following two examples:

```
>> round (2.574)
```

ans =

3

```
>> round (2.4)
```

ans =

2

The function *ceil* is demonstrated in the following two examples:

```
>> ceil (4.2)
```

ans =

5

```
>> ceil (4.8)
```

ans =

5

The function *floor* is demonstrated in the following two examples:

```
>> floor (4.2)
```

ans =

4

```
>> floor (4.8)
```

ans =

4

The *fix* function simply removes the fractional part of a real number:

```
» fix (5.789)
```

ans =

5

Complex Numbers

Operations on complex numbers are well implemented in MATLAB. MATLAB follows the convention that i or j represents the key value in complex analysis, the *imaginary number* $\sqrt{-1}$. All the usual arithmetic operators can be applied to complex numbers, and there are also some specific functions which have complex arguments. Both the real and the imaginary part of a complex number can be a real number or a symbolic constant, and operations with them are always performed in exact mode, unless otherwise instructed or necessary, in which case an approximation of the result is returned. As the imaginary unit is represented by the symbol i or j, the complex numbers are expressed in the form $a+bi$ or $a+bj$. Note that you don't need to use the product symbol (asterisk) before the imaginary unit:

```
>>  (1-5i)*(1-i)/(-1+2i)
```

ans =

-1.6000 + 2.8000i

```
>> format rat
>>  (1-5i) *(1-i) /(-1+2i)
```

ans =

-8/5 + 14/5i

Functions with Complex Arguments

Working with complex variables is very important in mathematical analysis and its many applications in engineering. MATLAB implements not only the usual arithmetic operations with complex numbers, but also various complex functions. The most important functions are listed below.

Trigonometric functions

Function	Inverse
sin (z)	asin (z)
cos (z)	acos (z)
tan (z)	atan(z) and atan2(imag(z),real(z))
csc (z)	acsc (z)
sec (z)	asec (z)
cot (z)	acot (z)

Hyperbolic functions

Function	Inverse
sinh (z)	asinh (z)
cosh(z)	acosh(z)
tanh(z)	atanh(z)
csch(z)	acsch(z)
sech(z)	asech(z)
coth (z)	acoth (z)

Exponential and logarithmic functions

Function	Meaning
exp (z)	*Exponential function in base e (e ^ z)*
log (z)	*Base e logarithm of z*
log10 (z)	*Base 10 logarithm of z.*
log2 (z)	*Base 2 logarithm of z.*
pow2 (z)	*2 to the power z.*
sqrt (z)	*The square root of z.*

Specific functions for the real and imaginary part

Function	Meaning
floor (z)	*Applies the floor function to real(z) and imag(z).*
ceil (z)	*Applies the ceil function to real(z) and imag(z).*
round (z)	*Applies the round function to real(z) and imag(z).*
fix (z)	*Applies the fix function to real(z) and imag(z).*

Specific functions for complex numbers

Function	Meaning
abs (z)	*The complex modulus of z.*
angle (z)	*The argument of z.*
conj (z)	*The complex conjugate of z.*
real (z)	*The real part of z.*
imag (z)	*The imaginary part of z.*

Below are some examples of operations with complex numbers.

```
>> round(1.5-3.4i)
```

ans =

2   -   3i

```
>> real(i^i)
```

ans =

0.2079

```
>>  (2+2i)^2/(-3-3*sqrt(3)*i)^90
```

ans =

0502e-085 - 1 + 7. 4042e-070i

```
>> sin (1 + i)
```

ans =

1.2985 + 0. 6350i

Elementary Functions that Support Complex Vector Arguments

MATLAB easily handles vector and matrix calculus. Indeed, its name, *MAtrix LABoratory*, already gives an idea of its power in working with vectors and matrices. MATLAB allows you to work with functions of a complex variable, but in addition this variable can even be a vector or a matrix. Below is a table of functions with complex vector arguments.

max (V)	*The maximum component of V. (max is calculated for complex vectors as the complex number with the largest complex modulus (magnitude), computed with max(abs(V)). Then it computes the largest phase angle with max(angle(x)), if necessary.)*
min (V)	*The minimum component of V. (min is calculated for complex vectors as the complex number with the smallest complex modulus (magnitude), computed with min(abs(A)). Then it computes the smallest phase angle with min(angle(x)), if necessary.)*
mean (V)	*Average of the components of V.*
median (V)	*Median of the components of V.*
std (V)	*Standard deviation of the components of V.*
sort (V)	*Sorts the components of V in ascending order. For complex entries the order is by absolute value and argument.*
sum (V)	*Returns the sum of the components of V.*
prod (V)	*Returns the product of the components of V, so, for example, n! = prod(1:n).*
cumsum (V)	*Gives the cumulative sums of the components of V.*
cumprod (V)	*Gives the cumulative products of the components of V.*
diff (V)	*Gives the vector of first differences of V (Vt - V-t-1).*
gradient (V)	*Gives the gradient of V.*
del2 (V)	*Gives the Laplacian of V (5-point discrete).*
fft (V)	*Gives the discrete Fourier transform of V.*
fft2 (V)	*Gives the two-dimensional discrete Fourier transform of V.*
ifft (V)	*Gives the inverse discrete Fourier transform of V.*
ifft2 (V)	*Gives the inverse two-dimensional discrete Fourier transform of V.*

These functions also support a complex matrix as an argument, in which case the result is a vector of column vectors whose components are the results of applying the function to each column of the matrix.

Here are some examples:

```
>> V = 2:7, W = [5 + 3i 2-i 4i]

V =

2    3    4    5    6    7

W =

2.0000 - 1.0000i        0 + 4.0000i   5.0000 + 3.0000i

>> diff(V), diff(W)

ans =

1    1    1    1    1

ans =

-2.0000 + 5.0000i   5.0000 - 1.0000i

>> cumprod(V), cumsum(V)

ans =

2    6    24    120    720    5040

ans =

2    5    9    14    20    27

>> cumsum(W), mean(W), std(W), sort(W), sum(W)

ans =

2.0000 - 1.0000i   2.0000 + 3.0000i   7.0000 + 6.0000i

ans =

2.3333 + 2.0000i

ans =

3.6515

ans =

2.0000 - 1.0000i 0 + 4.0000i   5.0000 + 3.0000i
```

```
ans =
```

```
7.0000 + 6.0000i
```

```
>> mean(V), std(V), sort(V), sum(V)
```

```
ans =
```

```
4.5000
```

```
ans =
```

```
1.8708
```

```
ans =
```

```
2    3    4    5    6    7
```

```
ans =
```

```
27
```

```
>> fft(W), ifft(W), fft2(W)
```

```
ans =
```

```
7.0000 + 6.0000i    0.3660 - 0.1699i   -1.3660 - 8.8301i
```

```
ans =
```

```
2.3333 + 2.0000i   -0.4553 - 2.9434i    0.1220 - 0.0566i
```

```
ans =
```

```
7.0000 + 6. 0000i 0.3660 - 0. 1699i - 1.3660 - 8. 8301i
```

Elementary Functions that Support Complex Matrix Arguments

- *Trigonometric*

sin (z)	*Sine function*
sinh (z)	*Hyperbolic sine function*
asin (z)	*Arcsine function*
asinh (z)	*Hyperbolic arcsine function*
cos (z)	*Cosine function*
cosh (z)	*Hyperbolic cosine function*

(*continued*)

acos (z)	*Arccosine function*
acosh (z)	*Hyperbolic arccosine function*
tan(z)	*Tangent function*
tanh (z)	*Hyperbolic tangent function*
atan (z)	*Arctangent function*
atan2 (z)	*Fourth quadrant arctangent function*
atanh (z)	*Hyperbolic arctangent function*
sec (z)	*Secant function*
sech (z)	*Hyperbolic secant function*
asec (z)	*Arccosecant function*
asech (z)	*Hyperbolic arccosecant function*
csc (z)	*Cosecant function*
csch (z)	*Hyperbolic cosecant function*
acsc (z)	*Arccosecant function*
acsch (z)	*Hyperbolic arccosecant function*
cot (z)	*Cotangent function*
coth (z)	*Hyperbolic cotangent function*
acot (z)	*Arccotangent function*
acoth (z)	*Hyperbolic arccotangent function*

- *Exponential*

exp (z)	*Base e exponential function*
log (z)	*Natural logarithm function (base e)*
log10 (z)	*Base 10 logarithm function*
sqrt (z)	*Square root function*

- *Complex*

abs (z)	*Modulus or absolute value*
angle (z)	*Argument*
conj (z)	*Complex conjugate*
imag (z)	*Imaginary part*
real (z)	*Real part*

- *Numerical*

fix (z)	*Removes the fractional part*
floor (z)	*Rounds to the nearest lower integer*
ceil (z)	*Rounds to the nearest greater integer*

(continued)

round (z)	*Performs common rounding*
rem (z1, z2)	*Returns the remainder of the division of z1 by z2*
sign (z)	*The sign of z*

- *Matrix*

expm (Z)	*Matrix exponential function by default*
expm1 (Z)	*Matrix exponential function in M-file*
expm2 (Z)	*Matrix exponential function via Taylor series*
expm3 (Z)	*Matrix exponential function via eigenvalues*
logm (Z)	*Logarithmic matrix function*
sqrtm (Z)	*Matrix square root function*
funm(Z,'function')	*Applies the function to the array Z*

Here are some examples:

```
>> A = [7 8 9; 1 2 3; 4 5 6], B = [1+2i 3+i;4+i,i]

A =

7    8    9
1    2    3
4    5    6

B =

1.0000 + 2.0000i   3.0000 + 1.0000i
4.0000 + 1.0000i        0 + 1.0000i

>> sin(A), sin(B), exp(A), exp(B), log(B), sqrt(B)

ans =

0.6570     0.9894     0.4121
0.8415     0.9093     0.1411
-0.7568    -0.9589    -0.2794

ans =

3.1658 + 1.9596i   0.2178 - 1.1634i
-1.1678 - 0.7682i       0 + 1.1752i

ans =

1.0e+003 *

1.0966     2.9810     8.1031
0.0027     0.0074     0.0201
0.0546     0.1484     0.4034
```

ans =

```
-1.1312 + 2.4717i   10.8523 +16.9014i
29.4995 +45.9428i    0.5403 + 0.8415i
```

ans =

```
0.8047 + 1.1071i   1.1513 + 0.3218i
1.4166 + 0.2450i        0 + 1.5708i
```

ans =

```
1.2720 + 0.7862i   1.7553 + 0.2848i
2.0153 + 0.2481i   0.7071 + 0.7071i
```

The exponential functions, square root and logarithm used above apply to the array elementwise and have nothing to do with the matrix exponential and logarithmic functions that are used below.

>> expm(B), logm(A), abs(B), imag(B)

ans =

```
-27.9191 +14.8698i -20.0011 +12.0638i
-24.7950 + 17.6831i-17.5059 + 14.0445i
```

ans =

```
11.9650 12.8038 - 19.9093
-21.7328-22.1157 44.6052
11.8921 12.1200 - 21.2040
```

ans =

```
2.2361 3.1623
4.1231 1.0000
```

ans =

```
2    1
1    1
```

>> fix(sin(B)), ceil(log(A)), sign(B), rem(A,3*ones(3))

ans =

```
3.0000 + 1.0000i        0 - 1.0000i
-1.0000                 0 + 1.0000i
```

ans =

```
2    3    3
0    1    2
2    2    2
```

ans =

```
0.4472 + 0.8944i    0.9487 + 0.3162i
0.9701 + 0.2425i         0 + 1.0000i
```

ans =

```
1    2    0
1    2    0
1    2    0
```

Random Numbers

MATLAB can easily generate (pseudo) random numbers. The function *rand* generates uniformly distributed random numbers and the function *randn* generates normally distributed random numbers. The most interesting features of MATLAB's random number generator are presented in the following table.

rand	*Returns a uniformly distributed random decimal number from the interval [0,1].*
rand (n)	*Returns an array of size n×n whose elements are uniformly distributed random decimal numbers from the interval [0,1].*
rand (m, n)	*Returns an array of dimension m×n whose elements are uniformly distributed random decimal numbers from the interval [0,1].*
rand (size (a))	*Returns an array of the same size as the matrix A and whose elements are uniformly distributed random decimal numbers from the interval [0,1].*
rand ('seed')	*Returns the current value of the uniform random number generator seed.*
rand('seed',n)	*Assigns to n the current value of the uniform random number generator seed.*
randn	*Returns a normally distributed random decimal number (mean 0 and variance 1).*
randn (n)	*Returns an array of dimension n×n whose elements are normally distributed random decimal numbers (mean 0 and variance 1).*
randn (m, n)	*Returns an array of dimension m×n whose elements are normally distributed random decimal numbers (mean 0 and variance 1).*
randn (size (a))	*Returns an array of the same size as the matrix A and whose elements are normally distributed random decimal numbers (mean 0 and variance 1).*
randn ('seed')	*Returns the current value of the normal random number generator seed.*
randn('seed',n)	*Assigns to n the current value of the uniform random number generator seed.*

Here are some examples:

```
>> [rand, rand (1), randn, randn (1)]
```

ans =

0.9501   0.2311   -0.4326   -1.6656

```
>> [rand(2), randn(2)]
```

ans =

0.6068   0.8913   0.1253   -1.1465
0.4860   0.7621   0.2877   1.1909

```
>> [rand(2,3), randn(2,3)]
```

ans =

0.3529 0.0099 0.2028   -0.1364 1.0668-0.0956
0.8132 0.1389 0.1987 0.1139 0.0593 - 0.8323

Operators

MATLAB features arithmetic, logical, relational, conditional and structural operators.

Arithmetic Operators

There are two types of arithmetic operators in MATLAB: matrix arithmetic operators, which are governed by the rules of linear algebra, and arithmetic operators on vectors, which are performed elementwise. The operators involved are presented in the following table.

Operator	Role played
+	*Sum of scalars, vectors, or matrices*
-	*Subtraction of scalars, vectors, or matrices*
*	*Product of scalars or arrays*
.*	*Product of scalars or vectors*
\	$A \backslash B = inv(A) * B$, where A and B are matrices
.\	$A. \backslash B = [B(i,j)/A(i,j)]$, where A and B are vectors $[dim(A) = dim(B)]$
/	*Quotient, or $B/A = B * inv(A)$, where A and B are matrices*
./	$A/B = [A(i,j)/b(i,j)]$, where A and B are vectors $[dim(A) = dim(B)]$
^	*Power of a scalar or matrix (M_p)*
.^	*Power of vectors $(A.^B = [A(i,j)^{B(i,j)}]$, for vectors A and B)*

Simple mathematical operations between scalars and vectors apply the scalar to all elements of the vector according to the defined operation, and simple operators between vectors are performed element by element. Below is the specification of these operators:

---

a = {a1, a2,..., an}, b = {b1, b2,..., bn}, c = scalar

a + c = [a1 +c, a2+ c,..., an+c]	*Sum of a scalar and a vector*
a * c = [a1 * c,a2* c ,..., an * c]	*Product of a scalar and a vector*
a + b = [a1+b1 a2+b2 ... an+bn]	*Sum of two vectors*
a. * b = [a1*b1 a2*b2 ... an*bn]	*Product of two vectors*
a. / b = [a1/b1 a2/b2 ... an/bn]	*Ratio to the right of two vectors*
a. \ b = [a1\b1 a2\b2 ... an\bn]	*Ratio to the left of two vectors*
a. ^ c = [a1 ^c, a2^ c ,..., an ^ c]	*Vector to the power of a scalar*
c. ^ a = [c ^ a1,c ^ a2,... ,c ^ an]	*Scalar to the power of a vector*
a.^b = [a1^b1 a2^b2 ... an^bn]	*Vector to the power of a vector*

It must be borne in mind that the vectors must be of the same length and that in the product, quotient and power the first operand must be followed by a point.

The following example involves all of the above operators.

```
>> X = [5,4,3]; Y = [1,2,7]; a = X + Y, b = X-Y, c = x * Y, d = 2. * X,...
e = 2/X, f = 2. \Y, g = x / Y, h =. \X, i = x ^ 2, j = 2. ^ X, k = X. ^ Y
```

a =

6   6   10

b =

4   2   -4

c =

5   8   21

d =

10   8   6

e =

0.4000   0.5000   0.6667

f =

0.5000   1.0000   3.5000

```
g =

5.0000    2.0000    0.4286

h =

5.0000    2.0000    0.4286

i =

25    16     9

j =

32 16 8

k =

5  16  2187
```

The above operations are all valid since in all cases the variable operands are of the same dimension, so the operations are successfully carried out element by element. For the sum and the difference there is no distinction between vectors and matrices, as the operations are identical in both cases.

The most important operators for matrix variables are specified below:

A + B, A - B, A * B	*Addition, subtraction and product of matrices.*
A\B	*If A is square, A\B = inv (A) * B. If A is not square, A\B is the solution, in the sense of least-squares, of the system AX = B.*
B/A	*Coincides with (A ' \ B')'.*
Aⁿ	*Coincides with A * A * A *... *A n times (n integer).*
pᴬ	*Performs the power operation only if p is a scalar.*

Here are some examples:

```
>> X = [5,4,3]; Y = [1,2,7]; l = X'* Y, m = X * Y ', n = 2 * X, o = X / Y, p = Y\X

l =

5  10  35
4  8  28
3  6  21

m =

34

n =

10  8  6
```

```
o =

0.6296

p =

0          0          0
0          0          0
0.7143  0.5714  0.4286
```

All of the above matrix operations are well defined since the dimensions of the operands are compatible in every case. We must not forget that a vector is a particular case of matrix, but to operate with it in matrix form (not element by element), it is necessary to respect the rules of dimensionality for matrix operations. For example, the vector operations $X.'*Y$ and $X.*Y'$ make no sense, since they involve vectors of different dimensions. Similarly, the matrix operations $X*Y, 2/X, 2\backslash Y, X^2, 2^X$ and X^Y make no sense, again because of a conflict of dimensions in the arrays.

Here are some more examples of matrix operators.

```
>> M = [1,2,3;1,0,2;7,8,9]

M =

1 2 3
1 0 2
7 8 9

>> B = inv (M), C = M ^ 2, D = M ^(1/2), E = 2 ^ M

B =

-0.8889     0.3333     0.2222
0.2778     -0.6667     0.0556
0.4444      0.3333    -0.1111

C =

24     26      34
15     18      21
78     86     118

D =

0.5219 + 0.8432i    0.5793 - 0.0664i    0.7756 - 0.2344i
0.3270 + 0.0207i    0.3630 + 1.0650i    0.4859 - 0.2012i
1.7848 - 0.5828i    1.9811 - 0.7508i    2.6524 + 0.3080i

E =

1. 0e + 003 *

0.8626 0.9568 1.2811
0.5401 0.5999 0.8027
2.9482 3.2725 4.3816
```

Relational Operators

MATLAB also provides relational operators. Relational operators perform element by element comparisons between two matrices and return an array of the same size whose elements are zero if the corresponding relationship is true, or one if the corresponding relation is false. The relational operators can also compare scalars with vectors or matrices, in which case the scalar is compared to all the elements of the array. Below is a table of these operators.

<	*Less than (for complex numbers this applies only to the real parts)*
< =	*Less than or equal (only applies to real parts of complex numbers)*
>	*Greater than (only applies to real parts of complex numbers)*
> =	*Greater than or equal (only applies to real parts of complex numbers)*
x == y	*Equality (also applies to complex numbers)*
x ~ = y	*Inequality (also applies to complex numbers)*

Logical Operators

MATLAB provides symbols to denote logical operators. The logical operators shown in the following table offer a way to combine or negate relational expressions.

~ A	*Logical negation (NOT) or the complement of A.*
A & B	*Logical conjunction (AND) or the intersection of A and B.*
A | B	*Logical disjunction (OR) or the union of A and B.*
XOR (A, B)	*Exclusive OR (XOR) or the symmetric difference of A and B (takes the value 1 if A or B, but not both, are 1).*

Here are some examples:

```
>> A = 2:7;P =(A>3) & (A<6)

P =

0    0    1    1    0    0
```

Returns 1 when the corresponding element of A is greater than 3 and less than 6, and returns 0 otherwise.

```
>> X = 3 * ones (3.3); X > = [7 8 9; 4 5 6 ; 1 2 3]

ans =

0 0 0
0 0 0
1 1 1
```

The elements of the solution array corresponding to those elements of X which are greater than or equal to the equivalent entry of the matrix *[7 8 9; 4 5 6 ; 1 2 3]* are assigned the value 1. The remaining elements are assigned the value 0.

Logical Functions

MATLAB implements logical functions whose output can take the value true (1) or false (0). The following table shows the most important logical functions.

exist(A)	*Checks if the variable or function exists (returns 0 if A does not exist and a number between 1 and 5, depending on the type, if it does exist).*
any(V)	*Returns 0 if all elements of the vector V are null and returns 1 if some element of V is non-zero.*
any(A)	*Returns 0 for each column of the matrix A with all null elements and returns 1 for each column of the matrix A which has non-null elements.*
all(V)	*Returns 1 if all the elements of the vector V are non-null and returns 0 if some element of V is null.*
all(A)	*Returns 1 for each column of the matrix A with all non-null elements and returns 0 for each column of the matrix A with at least one null element.*
find (V)	*Returns the places (or indices) occupied by the non-null elements of the vector V.*
isnan (V)	*Returns 1 for the elements of V that are indeterminate and returns 0 for those that are not.*
isinf (V)	*Returns 1 for the elements of V that are infinite and returns 0 for those that are not.*
isfinite (V)	*Returns 1 for the elements of V that are finite and returns 0 for those that are not.*
isempty (A)	*Returns 1 if A is an empty array and returns 0 otherwise (an empty array is an array such that one of its dimensions is 0).*
issparse (A)	*Returns 1 if A is a sparse matrix and returns 0 otherwise.*
isreal (V)	*Returns 1 if all the elements of V are real and 0 otherwise.*
isprime (V)	*Returns 1 for all elements of V that are prime and returns 0 for all elements of V that are not prime.*
islogical (V)	*Returns 1 if V is a logical vector and 0 otherwise.*
isnumeric (V)	*Returns 1 if V is a numeric vector and 0 otherwise.*
ishold	*Returns 1 if the properties of the current graph are retained for the next graph and only new elements will be added and 0 otherwise.*
isieee	*Returns 1 if the computer is capable of IEEE standard operations.*
isstr (S)	*Returns 1 if S is a string and 0 otherwise.*
ischart (S)	*Returns 1 if S is a string and 0 otherwise.*
isglobal (A)	*Returns 1 if A is a global variable and 0 otherwise.*
isletter (S)	*Returns 1 if S is a letter of the alphabet and 0 otherwise.*
isequal (A, B)	*Returns 1 if the matrices or vectors A and B are equal, and 0 otherwise.*
ismember(V, W)	*Returns 1 for every element of V which is in W and 0 for every element V that is not in W.*

Below are some examples using the above defined logical functions.

```
>> V = [1,2,3,4,5,6,7,8,9], isprime(V), isnumeric(V), all(V), any(V)

V =

1    2    3    4    5    6    7    8    9

ans =

0    1    1    0    1    0    1    0    0

ans =

1

ans =

1

ans =

1

>> B = [Inf, -Inf, pi, NaN], isinf(B), isfinite(B), isnan(B), isreal(B)

B =

Inf - Inf 3.1416 NaN

ans =

1 1 0 0

ans =

0 0 1 0

ans =

0 0 0 1

ans =

1

>> ismember ([1,2,3], [8,12,1,3]), A = [2,0,1];B = [4,0,2]; isequal (2A * B)

ans =

1 0 1

ans =

1
```

EXERCISE 2-1

Find the number of ways of choosing 12 elements from 30 without repetition, the remainder of the division of 2^{134} by 3, the prime decomposition of 18900, the factorial of 200 and the smallest number N which when divided by 16,24,30 and 32 leaves remainder 5.

```
>> factorial (30) / (factorial (12) * factorial(30-12))

ans =

8.6493e + 007
```

The command *vpa* is used to present the exact result.

```
>> vpa 'factorial (30) / (factorial (12) * factorial(30-12))' 15

ans =

86493225.
```

```
>> rem(2^134,3)

ans =

0
```

```
>> factor (18900)

ans =

2    2    3    3    3    5    5    7
```

```
>> factorial (100)

ans =

9. 3326e + 157
```

The command *vpa* is used to present the exact result.

```
>> vpa ' factorial (100)' 160

ans =

9332621544394415268169923885626670049071596826438162146859296389521759999322991560894146397615651828862536979208272237582511852109168640000000000000000000000000.
```

N-5 is the least common multiple of 16, 24, 30 and 32.

```
>> lcm (lcm (16.24), lcm (30,32))
```

ans =

480

Then N = 480 + 5 = 485.

EXERCISE 2-2

In base 5 find the result of the operation defined by $a25aaff6_{16}$ + $6789aba_{12}$ + 35671_8 + 1100221_3 - 1250. In base 13 find the result of the operation (666551_7)* $(aa199800a_{11})$ + $(fffaaa125_{16})$ / $(33331_4 + 6)$.

The result of the first operation in base 10 is calculated as follows:

```
>> base2dec('a25aaf6',16) + base2dec('6789aba',12) +...
base2dec('35671',8) + base2dec('1100221',3)-1250
```

ans =

190096544

We then convert this to base 5:

```
>> dec2base (190096544,5)
```

ans =

342131042134

Thus, the final result of the first operation in base 5 is 342131042134.

The result of the second operation in base 10 is calculated as follows:

```
>> base2dec('666551',7) * base2dec('aa199800a',11) +...
79 * base2dec('fffaaa125',16) / (base2dec ('33331', 4) + 6)
```

ans =

2. 7537e + 014

We now transform the result obtained into base 13.

```
>> dec2base (275373340490852,13)
```

ans =

BA867963C1496

EXERCISE 2-3

In base 13, find the result of the following operation:

$(666551_7)* (aa199800a_{11}) + (fffaaa125_{16}) / (33331_4 + 6).$

First, we perform the operation in base 10:

A more direct way of doing all of the above is:

```
>> base2dec('666551',7) * base2dec('aa199800a',11) +...
79 * base2dec('fffaaa125',16) / (base2dec ('33331', 4) + 6)
```

ans =

2. 753733404908515e + 014

We now transform the result obtained into base 13.

```
>> dec2base (275373340490852,13)
```

ans =

BA867963C1496

EXERCISE 2-4

Given the complex numbers $X = 2 + 2i$ and $Y=-3-3 \sqrt{3i}$, calculate Y^3 X^2/Y^{90}, $Y^{1/2}$, $Y^{3/2}$ and ln (X).

```
>> X=2+2*i; Y=-3-3*sqrt(3)*i;
>> Y^3
```

ans =

216

```
>> X ^ 2 / Y ^ 90
```

ans =

050180953422426e-085 - 1 + 7. 404188256695968e-070i

```
>> sqrt (Y)
```

ans =

1.22474487139159 - 2.12132034355964i

```
>> sqrt(Y^3)
```

ans =

14.69693845669907

```
>> log (X)
```

ans =

1.03972077083992 + 0.78539816339745i

EXERCISE 2-5

Calculate the value of the following operations with complex numbers:

$$\frac{i^8 - i^{-8}}{3 - 4i} + 1, \ i^{\sin(1+i)}, \ (2 + \ln(i))^{\frac{1}{i}}, \ (1+i)^i, \ i^{\ln(1+i)}, \ (1+\sqrt{3i})^{1-i}$$

```
>> (i^8-i^(-8))/(3-4*i) + 1
```

ans =

1

```
>> i^(sin(1+i))
```

ans =

-0.16665202215166 + 0.32904139450307i

```
>> (2+log(i))^(1/i)
```

ans =

1.15809185259777 - 1.56388053989023i

```
>> (1+i)^i
```

ans =

0.42882900629437 + 0.15487175246425i

```
>> i^(log(1+i))
```

ans =

0.24911518828716 + 0.15081974484717i

```
>>  (1+sqrt(3)*i)^(1-i)
```

ans =

5.34581479196611 + 1. 975948834528673i

EXERCISE 2-6

Calculate the real part, imaginary part, modulus and argument of each of the following expressions:

$$i^{3+i}, (1+\sqrt{3i})^{1-i}, i^{i^i}, i^i$$

```
>> Z1 = i ^ 3 * i; Z2 = (1 + sqrt (3) * i) ^(1-i); Z3 =(i^i) ^ i;Z4 = i ^ i;
```

```
>> format short
```

```
>> real ([Z1 Z2 Z3 Z4])
```

ans =

1.0000 5.3458 0.0000 0.2079

```
>> imag ([Z1 Z2 Z3 Z4])
```

ans =

0 1.9759 - 1.0000 0

```
>> abs ([Z1 Z2 Z3 Z4])
```

ans =

1.0000 5.6993 1.0000 0.2079

```
>> angle ([Z1 Z2 Z3 Z4])
```

ans =

0 0.3541 - 1.5708 0

EXERCISE 2-7

Generate a square matrix of order 4 whose elements are uniformly distributed random numbers from [0,1]. Generate another square matrix of order 4 whose elements are normally distributed random numbers from [0,1]. Find the present generating seeds, change their value to ½ and rebuild the two arrays of random numbers.

>> rand (4)

ans =

```
0.9501 0.8913 0.8214 0.9218
0.2311 0.7621 0.4447 0.7382
0.6068 0.4565 0.6154 0.1763
0.4860 0.0185 0.7919 0.4057
```

>> randn (4)

ans =

```
-0.4326-1.1465 0.3273 - 0.5883
-1.6656 1.1909 0.1746 2.1832
0.1253 1.1892-0.1867-0.1364
0.2877-0.0376 0.7258 0.1139
```

>> rand ('seed')

ans =

931316785

>> randn ('seed')

ans =

931316785

>> randn ('seed', 1/2)
>> rand ('seed', 1/2)
>> rand (4)

ans =

```
0.2190 0.9347 0.0346 0.0077
0.0470 0.3835 0.0535 0.3834
0.6789 0.5194 0.5297 0.0668
0.6793 0.8310 0.6711 0.4175
```

```
>> randn (4)
```

ans =

```
1.1650-0.6965 0.2641 1.2460
0.6268 1.6961 0.8717 -0.6390
0.0751 0.0591-1.4462 0.5774
0.3516 1.7971-0.7012-0.3600
```

EXERCISE 2-8

Given the vector variables a = [π, 2π, 3π, 4π, 5π] and b = [e, 2e, 3e, 4e, 5e], calculate c = sin (a) + b, d = cos (a), e = ln (b), f = c * d, g = c/d, h = d ^ 2, i = d ^ 2-e ^ 2 and j = 3d ^ 3-2e ^ 2.

```
>> a = [pi, 2 * pi, 3 * pi, 4 * pi, 5 * pi],
b = [exp (1), 2 * exp (1), 3 * exp (1), 4 * exp (1),5*exp(1)],
c=sin(a)+b,d=cos(a),e = log(b),f = c.*d,g = c./d,]
h=d.^2, i = d.^2-e.^2, j = 3*d.^3-2*e.^2
```

a =

```
3.1416    6.2832    9.4248    12.5664    15.7080
```

b =

```
2.7183 5.4366 8.1548 10.8731 13.5914
```

c =

```
2.7183 5.4366 8.1548 10.8731 13.5914
```
d =

```
-1     1     -1     1     -1
```

e =

```
1.0000 1.6931 2.0986 2.3863 2.6094
```

f =

```
-2.7183 5.4366 - 8.1548 10.8731 - 13.5914
```

g =

```
-2.7183 5.4366 - 8.1548 10.8731 - 13.5914
```

h =

    1   1   1   1   1

i =

    0 - 1.8667 - 3.4042 - 4.6944 - 5.8092

j =

    -5.0000 - 2.7335 - 11.8083 - 8.3888 - 16.6183

EXERCISE 2-9

Given a uniform random square matrix M of order 3, obtain its inverse, its transpose and its diagonal. Transform it into a lower triangular matrix (replacing the upper triangular entries by 0) and rotate it 90 degrees counterclockwise. Find the sum of the elements in the first row and the sum of the diagonal elements. Extract the subarray whose diagonal elements are at $_{11}$ and $_{22}$ and also remove the subarray whose diagonal elements are at $_{11}$ and $_{33}$.

```
>> M = rand(3)
```

M =

    0.6868   0.8462   0.6539
    0.5890   0.5269   0.4160
    0.9304   0.0920   0.7012

```
>> A = inv(M)
```
A =

    -4.1588   6.6947   -0.0934
     0.3255   1.5930   -1.2487
     5.4758   -9.0924   1.7138

```
>> B = M'
```

B =

    0.6868   0.5890   0.9304
    0.8462   0.5269   0.0920
    0.6539   0.4160   0.7012

```
>> V = diag(M)
```

V =

    0.6868
    0.5269
    0.7012

```
>> TI = tril(M)
```

TI =

```
0.6868        0          0
0.5890     0.5269        0
0.9304     0.0920     0.7012
```

```
>> TS = triu(M)
```

TS =

```
0.6868     0.8462     0.6539
0          0.5269     0.4160
0             0       0.7012
```

```
>> TR = rot90(M)
```

TR =

```
0.6539     0.4160     0.7012
0.8462     0.5269     0.0920
0.6868     0.5890     0.9304
```

```
>> s = M(1,1)+M(1,2)+M(1,3)
```
s =

2.1869

```
>> sd = M(1,1)+M(2,2)+M(3,3)
```

sd =

1.9149

```
>> SM = M(1:2,1:2)
```

SM =

```
0.6868 0.8462
0.5890 0.5269
```

```
>> SM1 = M([1 3], [1 3])
```

SM1 =

```
0.6868 0.6539
0.9304 0.7012
```

EXERCISE 2-10

Given the following complex square matrix M of order 3, find its square, its square root and its base 2 and − 2 exponential:

$$M = \begin{bmatrix} i & 2i & 3i \\ 4i & 5i & 6i \\ 7i & 8i & 9i \end{bmatrix}.$$

```
>> M = [i 2*i 3*i; 4*i 5*i 6*i; 7*i 8*i 9*i]
```

M =

```
0 + 1.0000i       0 + 2.0000i       0 + 3.0000i
0 + 4.0000i       0 + 5.0000i       0 + 6.0000i
0 + 7.0000i       0 + 8.0000i       0 + 9.0000i
```

```
>> C = M^2
```

C =

```
-30     -36     -42
-66     -81     -96
-102    -126    -150
```

```
>> D = M^(1/2)
```

D =

```
0.8570 - 0.2210i    0.5370 + 0.2445i    0.2169 + 0.7101i
0.7797 + 0.6607i    0.9011 + 0.8688i    1.0224 + 1.0769i
0.7024 + 1.5424i    1.2651 + 1.4930i    1.8279 + 1.4437i
```

```
>> 2^M
```

ans =

```
0.7020 - 0.6146i   -0.1693 - 0.2723i   -0.0407 + 0.0699i
-0.2320 - 0.3055i    0.7366 - 0.3220i   -0.2947 - 0.3386i
-0.1661 + 0.0036i   -0.3574 - 0.3717i    0.4513 - 0.7471i
```

```
>> (-2)^M
```

ans =

```
17.3946 -16.8443i    4.3404 - 4.5696i   -7.7139 + 7.7050i
1.5685 - 1.8595i    1.1826 - 0.5045i   -1.2033 + 0.8506i
-13.2575 +13.1252i   -3.9751 + 3.5607i    6.3073 - 6.0038i
```

EXERCISE 2-11

Given the complex matrix M in the previous exercise, find its elementwise logarithm and its elementwise base e exponential. Also calculate the results of the matrix operations e^M and ln (M).

```
>> M = [i 2*i 3*i; 4*i 5*i 6*i; 7*i 8*i 9*i]
```

```
>> log(M)
```

ans =

```
     0 + 1.5708i    0.6931 + 1.5708i    1.0986 + 1.5708i
1.3863 + 1.5708i    1.6094 + 1.5708i    1.7918 + 1.5708i
1.9459 + 1.5708i    2.0794 + 1.5708i    2.1972 + 1.5708i
```

```
>> exp(M)
```

ans =

```
0.5403 + 0.8415i   -0.4161 + 0.9093i  -0.9900 + 0.1411i
-0.6536 - 0.7568i   0.2837 - 0.9589i   0.9602 - 0.2794i
0.7539 + 0.6570i   -0.1455 + 0.9894i  -0.9111 + 0.4121i
```

```
>> logm(M)
```

ans =

```
-5.4033 - 0.8472i   11.9931 - 0.3109i   -5.3770 + 0.8846i
12.3029 + 0.0537i  -22.3087 + 0.8953i   12.6127 + 0.4183i
-4.7574 + 1.6138i   12.9225 + 0.7828i   -4.1641 + 0.6112i
```

```
>> expm(M)
```

ans =

```
0.3802 - 0.6928i   -0.3738 - 0.2306i   -0.1278 + 0.2316i
-0.5312 - 0.1724i    0.3901 - 0.1434i   -0.6886 - 0.1143i
-0.4426 + 0.3479i   -0.8460 - 0.0561i   -0.2493 - 0.4602i
```

EXERCISE 2-12

Given the complex vector V = [1 + i, i, 1-i], find the mean, median, standard deviation, variance, sum, product, maximum and minimum of its elements, as well as its gradient, its discrete Fourier transform and its inverse discrete Fourier transform.

>> [mean(V),median(V),std(V),var(V),sum(V),prod(V),max(V),min(V)]'

ans =

0.6667 - 0.3333i
1.0000 + 1.0000i
1.2910
1.6667
2.0000 - 1.0000i
0 - 2.0000i
1.0000 + 1.0000i
0 - 1.0000i

>> **gradient(V)**

ans =

1.0000 - 2.0000i 0.5000 0 + 2.0000i

>> **fft(V)**

ans =

2.0000 + 1.0000i -2.7321 + 1.0000i 0.7321 + 1.0000i

>> **ifft(V)**

ans =

0.6667 + 0. 3333i 0.2440 + 0. 3333i - 0.9107 + 0. 3333i

EXERCISE 2-13

Given the arrays

$$A = \begin{bmatrix} 1 & 1 & 0 \\ 0 & 1 & 1 \\ 0 & 0 & 1 \end{bmatrix} \quad B = \begin{bmatrix} i & 1-i & 2+i \\ 0 & -1 & 3-i \\ 0 & 0 & -i \end{bmatrix} \quad C = \begin{bmatrix} 1 & 1 & 1 \\ 0 & sqrt(2)i & -sqrt(2)i \\ 1 & -1 & -1 \end{bmatrix}$$

calculate AB – BA, A^2 + B^2 + C^2, ABC, sqrt (A)+sqrt(B)+sqrt(C), $e^A(e^B+ e^C)$, their transposes and their inverses. Also verify that the product of any of the matrices A, B, C with its inverse yields the identity matrix.

```
>> A = [1 1 0;0 1 1;0 0 1]; B = [i 1-i 2+i;0 -1 3-i;0 0 -i]; C = [1 1 1; 0 sqrt(2)*i
-sqrt(2)*i;1 -1 -1];
```

```
>> M1 = A*B-B*A
```

M1 =

```
0              -1.0000 - 1.0000i   2.0000
0                     0            1.0000 - 1.0000i
0                     0                   0
```

```
>> M2 = A^2+B^2+C^2
```

M2 =

```
2.0000          2.0000 + 3.4142i   3.0000 - 5.4142i
0 - 1.4142i    -0.0000 + 1.4142i   0.0000 - 0.5858i
0               2.0000 - 1.4142i   2.0000 + 1.4142i
```

```
>> M3 = A*B*C
```

M3 =

```
5.0000 + 1.0000i   -3.5858 + 1.0000i   -6.4142 + 1.0000i
3.0000 - 2.0000i   -3.0000 + 0.5858i   -3.0000 + 3.4142i
0 - 1.0000i         0 + 1.0000i         0 + 1.0000i
```

```
>> M4 = sqrtm(A)+sqrtm(B)-sqrtm(C)
```

M4 =

```
0.6356 + 0.8361i   -0.3250 - 0.8204i   3.0734 + 1.2896i
0.1582 - 0.1521i    0.0896 + 0.5702i   3.3029 - 1.8025i
-0.3740 - 0.2654i   0.7472 + 0.3370i   1.2255 + 0.1048i
```

```
>> M5 = expm(A)*(expm(B)+expm(C))
```

M5 =

```
14.1906 - 0.0822i   5.4400 + 4.2724i   17.9169 - 9.5842i
4.5854 - 1.4972i    0.6830 + 2.1575i   8.5597 - 7.6573i
3.5528 + 0.3560i    0.1008 - 0.7488i   3.2433 - 1.8406i
```

```
>> inv(A)
```

ans =

```
1 1  1
0 1 -1
0 0  1
```

```
>> inv(B)
```

ans =

```
0 - 1.0000i  -1.0000 - 1.0000i  -4.0000 + 3.0000i
0               -1.0000          1.0000 + 3.0000i
0                 0              0 + 1.0000i
```

```
>> inv(C)
```

ans =

```
0.5000   0                   0.5000
0.2500   0   -0.3536i   -0.2500
0.2500   0   +0.3536i   -0.2500
```

```
>> [A*inv(A) B*inv(B) C*inv(C)]
```

ans =

```
1   0   0   1   0   0   1   0   0
0   1   0   0   1   0   0   1   0
0   0   1   0   0   1   0   0   1
```

```
>> A'
```

ans =

```
1 0 0
1 1 0
0 1 1
```

```
>> B'
```

ans =

```
0 - 1.0000i           0                    0
1.0000 + 1.0000i  -1.0000                  0
2.0000 - 1.0000i   3.0000 + 1.0000i    0 + 1.0000i
```

```
>> C'
```

ans =

```
1.0000   0                  1.0000
1.0000   0   -1.4142i   -1.0000
1.0000   0   +1.4142i   -1.0000
```

CHAPTER 3

■ ■ ■

Control Systems

Introduction to Control Systems

MATLAB offers an integrated environment in which you can design control systems. The diagram in Figure 3-1 shows how an engineering problem leads to the development of models and the analysis of experimental data, which in turn lead to the design and simulation of control systems. The subsequent analysis of these systems leads to further modifications of the design, this development loop resulting in rapid prototyping and implementation of effective systems.

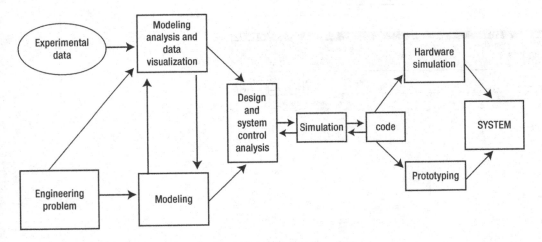

Figure 3-1.

MATLAB provides a high-level platform for technical model generation, data analysis and algorithm development. MATLAB combines comprehensive engineering and mathematics functionality with powerful visualization and animation features, all within a high-level interactive programming language. The MATLAB toolboxes extend the MATLAB environment to incorporate a wide range of classical and modern techniques for the design of control systems, providing cutting edge control algorithms developed by internationally recognized experts.

MATLAB contains more than 600 mathematical, statistical and engineering functions, providing the power of numerical calculation you need to analyze data, develop algorithms and optimize the performance of a system. With MATLAB, you can run fast iterations of designs and compare performances of alternative control strategies. In addition, MATLAB is a high-level programming language that allows you to develop algorithms in a fraction of the time spent in *C*, *C++* or FORTRAN. MATLAB is open and extendible, you can see the source code, modify algorithms and incorporate existing *C*, *C++* and FORTRAN programs.

The interactive *Control System Toolbox* tools facilitate the design and adjustment of control systems. For example, you might drag poles and zeros and see immediately how the system reacts (Figure 3-2). In addition, MATLAB provides powerful interactive 2-D and 3-D graphics features showing data, equations, and results (Figure 3-3). It is possible to use a wide range of visualization aids in MATLAB or you can take advantage of the specific control functions which are provided by the MATLAB toolboxes.

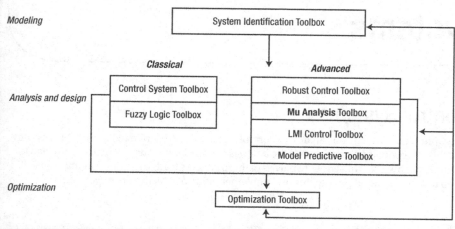

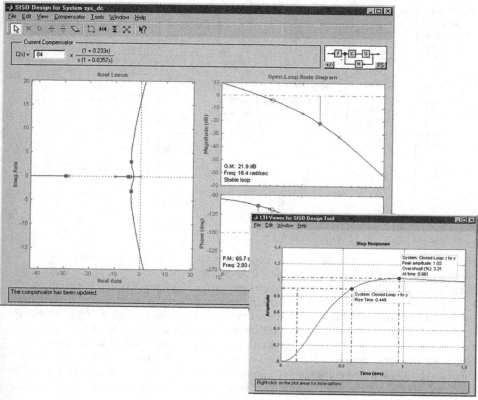

Figure 3-2.

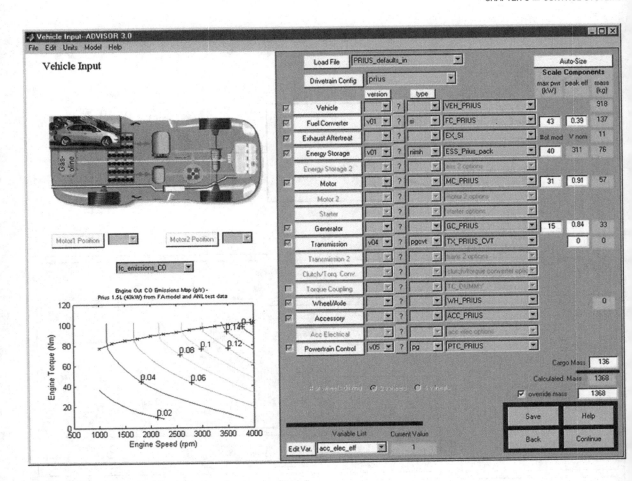

Figure 3-3.

The MATLAB toolboxes include applications written with MATLAB language-specific functionality. The MATLAB control-related toolboxes encompass virtually all of the fundamental techniques of control design, from LQG and root-locus to H and logical diffuse methods. For example, it might add a fuzzy logic control system design using the built-in algorithms of the *Fuzzy Logic Toolbox* (Figure 3-4).

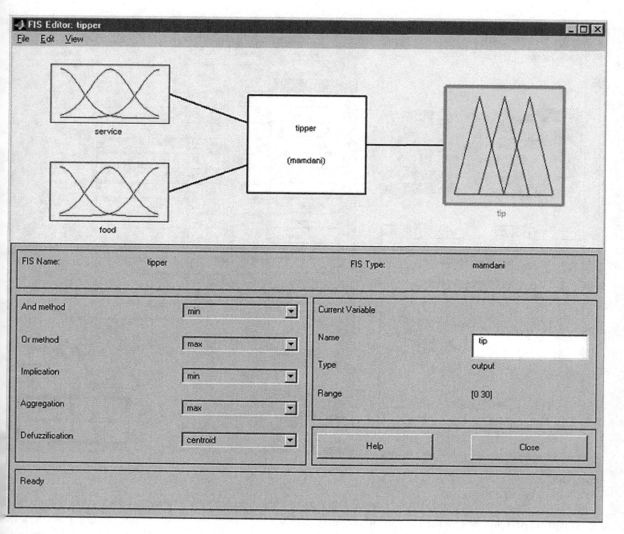

Figure 3-4.

The most important MATLAB toolboxes for control systems can be classified into three families: modeling (*System Identification Toolbox*), classical design and analysis products (*Control System Toolbox* and *Fuzzy Logic Toolbox*), design and advanced analysis products (*Robust Control Toolbox, Mu-Analysis Toolbox, LMI Control Toolbox* and *Model Predictive Toolbox*) and optimization products (*Optimization Toolbox*). The following diagram illustrates this classification.

Control System Design and Analysis: The Control System Toolbox

The *Control System Toolbox* is a collection of algorithms, mainly written as M-files, that implement common techniques of design, analysis, and modeling of control systems. Its wide range of services includes classical and modern methods of control design, including root locus, pole placement and LQG regulator design. Certain graphical user interfaces simplify the typical tasks of control engineering. This toolbox is built on the fundamentals of MATLAB to facilitate specialized control systems for engineering tools.

With the *Control System Toolbox* you can create models of linear time-invariant systems (LTI) in transfer function, zero-pole-gain or state-space formats. You can manipulate both discrete-time and continuous-time systems and convert between various representations. You can calculate and graph time response, frequency response and loci of roots. Other functions allow you to perform placement of poles, optimal control and estimates. The *Control System Toolbox* is open and extendible, allowing you to create customized M-files to suit your specific applications.

The following are the key features of the *Control System Toolbox*:

- *LTI Viewer*: An interactive GUI to analyze and compare LTI systems.

- *SISO Design Tool*: An interactive GUI to analyze and adjust single-input/single-output (SISO) feedback control systems.

- *GUI Suite*: Sets preferences and properties to give full control over the display of time and frequency plots.

- *LTI objects*: Structures specialized data to concisely represent model data in transfer function, state-space, zero-pole-gain and frequency response formats.

- MIMO: Support for multiple-input/multiple-output (MIMO) systems, sampled data, continuous-time systems and systems with time delay.

- *Functions and operators to connect LTI models*: Creates complex block diagrams (connections in series, parallel and feedback).

- Support for various methods of converting discrete systems to continuous systems, and vice versa.

- Functions to graphically represent solutions for time and frequency systems and compare various systems with a single command.

- Tools for classical and modern techniques of control design, including root locus analysis, loop shaping, pole placement and LQR/LQG control.

Construction of Models

The *Control System Toolbox* supports the representation of four linear models: state-space models (SS), transfer functions (TF), zero-pole-gain models (ZPK) and frequency data models (FRD). LTI objects are provided for each model type. In addition to model data, LTI objects can store the sample time of discrete-time systems, delays, names of inputs and outputs, notes on the model and many other details. Using LTI objects, you can manipulate models as unique entities and combine them using matrix-type operations. An illustrative example of the design of a simple LQG controller is shown in Figure 3-5. The code extract at the bottom shows how the controller is designed and how the closed-loop system has been created. The plot of the frequency response shows a comparison between the open-loop system (red) and closed loop system (blue).

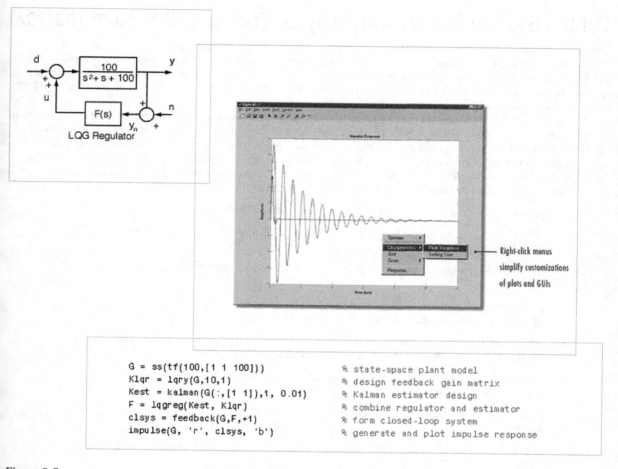

Figure 3-5.

The *Control System Toolbox* contains commands which analyze and compute model features such as I/O dimensions, poles, zeros and DC gain. These commands apply both to continuous-time and discrete-time models.

Analysis and Design

Some tasks lend themselves to graphic manipulation, while others benefit from the flexibility of the command line. The *Control System Toolbox* is designed to accommodate both approaches, providing a complete set of functions for the design and analysis of models via the command line or GUI.

Graphical Analysis of Models Using the LTI Viewer

The *Control System Toolbox* LTI Viewer is a GUI that simplifies the analysis of linear time-invariant systems (it is loaded by typing >>ltiview in the command window). The LTI Viewer is used to simultaneously view and compare the response plots of several linear models. It is possible to generate time and frequency response plots and to inspect key response parameters such as time of ascent, maximum overshooting and stability margins. Using mouse-driven interactions, you can select input and output channels for MIMO systems. The LTI Viewer can simultaneously display up to six different types of plots including step, impulse, *Bode* (magnitude and phase or magnitude only), *Nyquist*, *Nichols*, sigma, and pole/zero. Right-clicking will reveal an options menu which gives you access to several controls and LTI Viewer Options, including:

- **Plot Type:** Change the type of plot.

- **Systems:** Selects or deselects any of the models loaded in the LTI Viewer.

- **Characteristics:** Displays parameters and key response characteristics.

- **Zoom:** Enlargement and reduction of parts of the plot.

- **Grid:** Add grids to the plots.

- **Properties:** Opens the *Property Editor*, where you can customize attributes of the plot.

In addition to the right-click menu, all the response plots include data markers. These allow you to scan the plot data, identify key data and determine the system font for a given plot. Using the LTI Viewer you can easily graphically represent solutions for one or several systems using step response plots, zero/pole plots and all frequency response plots (*Bode, Nyquist, Nichols* and singular values plots), all in a single window (see Figure 3-6). The LTI Viewer allows you to display important response characteristics in the plots, such as margins of stability, using data markers.

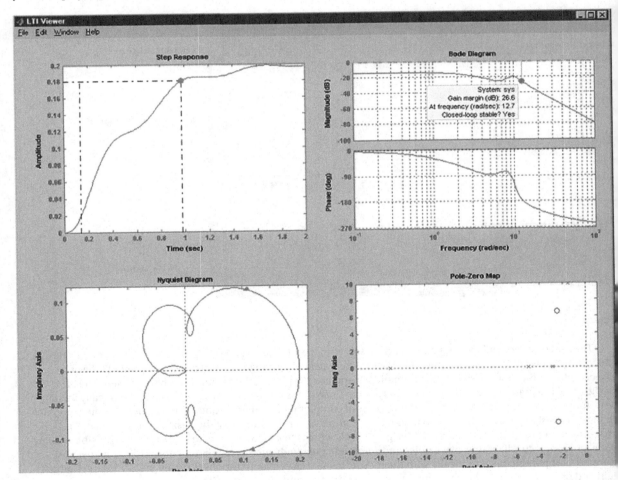

Figure 3-6.

Analysis of Models Using the Command Line

The LTI Viewer is suitable for a wide range of applications where you want a GUI-driven environment. For situations that require programming, custom plots or data unrelated to their LTI models, the *Control System Toolbox* provides command line functions that perform the basic frequency plots and time domain analysis used in control systems engineering. These functions apply to any type of linear model (continuous or discontinuous, SISO or MIMO) or arrays of models.

Compensator Design Using the SISO Design Tool

The *Control System Toolbox* SISO Design Tool is a GUI that allows you to analyze and adjust SISO control feedback systems (loaded by typing >>*sisotool* in the command window). Using the SISO Design Tool, you can graphically adjust the dynamics and the compensator gain using a mixture of root locus and loop shaping techniques. For example, you can use the view of the locus of the roots to stabilize a feedback loop and force a minimum buffer, and use Bode diagrams to adjust bandwidth, gain and phase margins or add a filter *notch* to reject disturbances. The SISO Design GUI can be used for continuous-time and discrete-time time plants. Figure 3-7 shows root locus and Bode diagrams for a discrete-time plant.

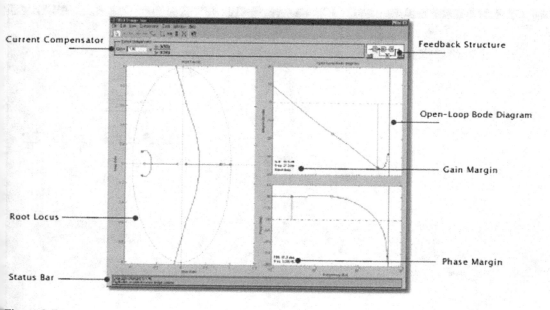

Figure 3-7.

The SISO Design Tool is designed to work closely with the LTI Viewer, allowing you to quickly reiterate a design and immediately see the results in the LTI Viewer. When making a change to the compensator, the LTI Viewer associated with the SISO Design Tool automatically updates the plots of the solution you have chosen. The SISO Design Tool integrates most of the functionality of the *Control System Toolbox* in a single GUI, dynamically linking time, frequency, and pole/zero plots, offering views of complementary themes and design goals, providing graphical changes in Design view and helping to manage the complexity and iterations of the design. The right-click and drop-down menus give you flexibility to design controls with a click of the mouse. In particular, it is possible to view Bode and root locus diagrams, place poles and zeros, add delay/advance networks and notch filters, adjust the compensator parameters graphically with the mouse, inspect closed loop responses (using the LTI Viewer), adjust gain and phase margins and convert models between discrete and continuous time.

Compensator Design Using the Command Line

In addition to the SISO Design Tool, the *Control System Toolbox* provides a number of commands that can be used for a wider range of control applications, including functions for classical SISO design (data buffer, locus of the roots and gain and phase margins) and functions for modern MIMO design (placement of poles, LQR/LQG methods and Kalman filtering). Linear-Quadratic-Gaussian (LQG) control is a modern state-space technique used for the design of optimal dynamic regulators, allowing the balance of benefits of regulation and control costs, taking into account perturbations of the process and measuring noise.

The Control System Toolbox Commands

The *Control System Toolbox* commands can be classified according to their purpose as follows:

General

Ctrlpref: Opens a GUI which allows you to change the *Control System Toolbox* preferences (see Figure 3-8).

Creation of linear models

tf: Creates a transfer function model
zpk: Creates a zero-pole-gain model
ss: Creates a state-space model
dss: Creates a descriptor state-space model
frd: Creates a frequency-response data model
set: Locates and modifies properties of LTI models

Data extraction

tfdata: Accesses transfer function data (in particular extracts the numerator and denominator of the transfer function)
zpkdata: Accesses zero-pole-gain data
ssdata: Accesses state-space model data
get: Accesses properties of LTI models

Conversions

s: Converts to a state-space model
zpk: Converts to a zero-pole-gain model
tf: Converts to a transfer function model
frd: Converts to a frequency-response data model
c2d: Converts a model from continuous to discrete time
d2c: Converts a model from discrete to continuous time
d2d: Resamples a discrete time model

System interconnection

append: Groups models by appending their inputs and outputs
parallel: Parallel connection of two models
series: Series connection of two models
feedback: Connection feedback of two systems
lft: Generalized feedback interconnection of two models
connect: Block diagram interconnection of dynamic systems

(*continued*

Dynamic models

iopzmap: Plots a pole-zero map for input/output pairs of a model
bandwidth: Returns the frequency-response bandwidth of the system
pole: Computes the poles of a dynamic system
zero: Returns the zeros and gain of a SISO dynamic system
pzmap: Returns a pole-zero plot of a dynamic system
damp: Returns the natural frequency and damping ratio of the poles of a system
dcgain: Returns the low frequency (DC) gain of an LTI system
norm: Returns the norm of a linear model
covar: Returns the covariance of a system driven by white noise

Time-domain analysis

ltiview: An LTI viewer for LTI system response analysis
step: Produces a step response plot of a dynamic system
impulse: Produces an impulse response plot of a dynamic system
initial: Produces an initial condition response plot of a state-space model
lsim: Simulates the time response of a dynamic system to arbitrary inputs

Frequency-domain analysis

ltiview: An LTI viewer for LTI system response analysis
bode: Produces a Bode plot of frequency response, magnitude and phase of frequency response
sigma: Produces a singular values plot of a dynamic system
nyquist: Produces a Nyquist plot of frequency response
nichols: Produces a Nichols chart of frequency response
margin: Returns gain margin, phase margin, and crossover frequencies
allmargin: Returns gain margin, phase margin, delay margin and crossover frequencies
freqresp: Returns frequency response over a grid

Classic design

sisotool: Interactively design and tune SISO feedback loops (technical *root locus* and *loop shaping*)
rlocus: Root locus plot of a dynamic system

Pole placement

place: MIMO pole placement design
estim: Forms a state estimator given estimator gain
reg: Forms a regulator given state-feedback and estimator gains

LQR/LQG design

lqr: Linear quadratic regulator (LQR) design
dlqr: Linear-quadratic (LQ) state-feedback regulator for a discrete-time state-space system
lqry: Linear-quadratic (LQ) state-feedback regulator with output weighting
lqrd: Discrete linear-quadratic (LQ) regulator for a continuous plant
Kalman: Kalman estimator
kalmd: Discrete Kalman estimator for a continuous plant

(*continued*)

State-space models

rss: Generates a random continuous test model
drss: Generates a random discrete test model
ss2ss: State coordinate transformation for state-space models
ctrb: Controllability matrix
obsv: Observability matrix
gram: Control and observability gramians
minreal: Minimal realization or pole-zero cancelation
ssbal: Balance state-space models using a diagonal similarlity transformation
balreal: Gramian-based input/output balancing of state-space realizations
modred: Model order reduction

Models with time delays

totaldelay: Total combined input/output delay for an LTI model
delay2z: Replaces delays of discrete-time TF, SS, or ZPK models by poles at z=0, or replaces delays of FRD models [Note: in more recent versions of MATLAB, *delay2z* has been replaced with *absorbDelay*.]
pade: Padé approximation of a model with time delays

Matrix equation solvers

lyap: Solves continuous-time Lyapunov equations
dlyap: Solves discrete-time Lyapunov equations
care: Solves continuous-time algebraic Riccati equations
dare: Solves discrete-time algebraic Riccati equations

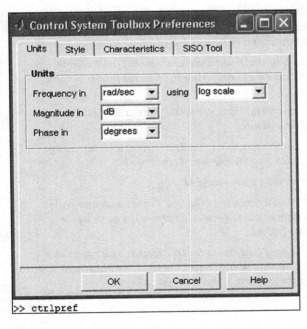

Figure 3-8.

The following sections present the syntax of the above commands, appropriately grouped into the previously mentioned categories.

LTI Model Commands

Command	Description
sys = drss(n, m, p)	Generates a random discrete-time state-space model of order n with m inputs and p outputs.
sys = drss(n, p)	Equivalent to drss(n,m,p) with m = 1.
sys = drss(n)	Equivalent to drss(n,m,p) with n = m = 1.
sys = drss(n,m,p,s1,...sn)	Generates an array of state-space models.
dss (A,B,C,D,E)	Creates the continuous-time descriptor state-space model: $$E\frac{dx}{dt} = Ax + Bu$$ $$y = Cx + Du$$
dss (A,B,C,D,E, Ts)	Creates the discrete -time descriptor state-space model (with sample time Ts in seconds): $$Ex[n+1] = Ax[n]Bu[n]$$ $$y[n] = Cx[n] + Du[n]$$
dss (A,B,C,D,E, ltisys)	Creates the descriptor state-space model with generic LTI properties inherited from the model ltisys.
dss (A,B,C,D,E, p1, p2, v1, v2,...)	Creates the continuous-time descriptor state-space model with generic LTI properties given by the propery/value pairs (pi, vi).
dss (A,B,C,D,E, Ts, p2, p1, v1, v2,...)	Creates the discrete-time descriptor state-space model (with sample time Ts in seconds) with generic LTI properties given by the property/value pairs (pi, vi).
sys = filt(num,den)	Creates a discrete transfer function in the DSP format with numerator num and denominator den.
sys = filt(num,den,Ts)	Creates a discrete transfer function in the DSP format with numerator num, denominator den and sample time Ts in seconds.
sys = filt (M)	Specifies a static filter with gain matrix M.
sys = filt(num,den, p1,v1,p2,v2,...)	Creates a discrete transfer function in the DSP format with numerator num and denominator den and generic LTI properties given by the property/value pairs (pi, vi).
sys = filt(num,den,Ts, p1,v1,p2,v2,...)	Creates a discrete transfer function in the DSP format with numerator num and denominator den, sample time Ts in seconds, and generic LTI properties given by the property/value pairs (pi, vi).

(continued)

Command	Description
sys = frd(r,f)	Creates a frequency-response data (FRD) model from the frequency response data stored in r, where f represents the underlying frequencies for the frequency response data.f
sys = frd(r,f,Ts)	Creates a frequency-response data model with scalar sample time Ts in seconds.
sys = frd	Creates an empty frequency-response data model.
sys = frd(r,f,ltisys)	Creates a frequency-response data model object with generic LTI properties inherited from the model ltisys.
sysfrd = frd(sys,f)	Converts a TF, SS, or ZPK model to an FRD model with frequency samples given by f.
sysfrd = frd(sys,f,u)	Converts a TF, SS, or ZPK model to an FRD model with frequency samples given by f in units specified by the string u (for example 'rad/s' or 'Hz').
[r,f] = frdata(sys)	Returns the response data and frequency samples of the FRD model sys.
[r,f,Ts] = frdata(sys)	Returns the response data, frequency samples and sample time of the FRD model sys.
[r,f] = frdata(sys,'v')	Returns the response data and frequency samples of the FRD model sys directly as column vectors.
get(sys)	Displays all the properties and values of the FRD model sys.
get(sys, 'P')	Displays the current value of the property name P of the FRD model sys.
sys = rss(n,m,p)	Generates a random continuous test model of order n with m inputs and p outputs.
sys = rss(n,p)	Equivalent to rss(n,m,p) with m = 1.
sys = rss(n)	Equivalent to rss(n,m,p) with n = m = 1.
sys = rss(n,m,p,s1,...sn)	Generates an s1×...×sn array of nth order state-space models with m inputs and p outputs.
set(sys,'P',V)	Assigns the value V to the given property of the LTI model sys.
set(sys,'P1','V1','P2','V2',...)	Allocates values V1,...,VN to the properties P1,...,PN of the LTI model sys.
set(sys,'P')	Returns the permissible values for the property P.
set(sys)	Displays all sys properties and their values.
ss (A,B,C,D,E).	Creates the continuous-time state-space model: $$E\frac{dx}{dt} = Ax + Bu$$ $$y = Cx + Du$$
ss (A,B,C,D,E, Ts)	Creates the discrete-time state-space model (with sample time Ts in seconds): $$Ex[n+1] = Ax[n]Bu[n]$$ $$y[n] = Cx[n] + Du[n]$$
ss (D)	Equivalent to ss([],[],[],D).

(continued

Command	Description
ss (A,B,C,D,E, ltisys)	Creates a state-space model with generic LTI properties inherited from the model ltisys.
ss (A,B,C,D,E, p1, p2, v1, v2,...)	Creates a state-space model with properties given by the property/value pairs (pi, vi).
ss (a, b, c, d, e, Ts, p2, p1, v1, v2,...)	Creates a discrete state-space model with properties given by the property/value pairs (pi, vi)) and sample time Ts in seconds.
sys_ss = ss(sys)	Converts the (TF or ZPK) model sys to a state-space model.
sys_ss = ss(sys,'minimal')	produces a state-space realization with no uncontrollable or unobservable states.
[A,B,C,D] = ssdata(sys)	Extracts the model data [A, B, C, D] from the state-space model sys.
[A,B,C,D,Ts] = ssdata(sys)	Extracts the model data [A, B, C, D] and the sample time Ts from the state-space model sys.
[A,B,C,D] = dssdata(sys)	Extracts the model data [A, B, C, D] from the descriptor state-space model sys.
[A,B,C,D,Ts] = dssdata(sys)	Extracts the model data [A, B, C, D] and the sample time Ts from the descriptor state-space model sys.
sys = tf(num,den)	Creates a continuous-time transfer function with specified numerator and denominator.
sys = tf(num,den,Ts)	Creates a discrete-time transfer function with specified numerator and denominator and sample of Ts time in seconds.
sys = tf (M)	Creates a static gain M (matrix or scalar).
sys = tf(num,den,ltisys)	Creates a transfer function with specified numerator and denominator and generic properties inherited from the LTI model ltisys.
sys = tf(num,den, p1,v1,p2,v2,...)	Creates a continuous-time transfer function with specified numerator and denominator and with properties given by the property/value pairs (pi, vi).
sys = tf(num,den,Ts, p1,v1,p2,v2,...)	Creates a discrete-time transfer function with specified numerator and denominator, sample time Ts in seconds, and properties given by the property/value pairs (pi, vi).
s = tf('s')	Specifies a TF model using a rational function in the Laplace variable s.
z = tf('z',Ts)	Specifies a TF model with sample time Ts using a rational function in the discrete-time variable z.
tfsys = tf(sys)	Converts a (TF or ZPK) model sys to a transfer function.
tfsys = tf(sys,'inv')	Converts a (TF or ZPK) model sys to a transfer function using investment formulas.
[num,den] = tfdata(sys)	Returns the numerator and denominator for type TF, SS, or ZPK sys transfer function models.
[num,den] = tfdata(sys,'v')	Returns the numerator and denominator as row vectors.
[num,den,Ts] = tfdata(sys)	In addition to the above, also returns sample time Ts.
TD = totaldelay (sys)	Gives the combined total input/output lag of the LTI model sys

(continued)

Command	Description
sys = zpk (z, p, k)	*Creates a continuous-time zero-pole-gain model with zeros z, poles p and gains k.*
sys = zpk (z, p, k, Ts)	*Creates a discrete-time zero-pole-gain model with zeros z, poles p, gains k and sample time Ts in seconds.*
sys = zpk(M)	*Specifies a static gain M.*
sys = zpk(z,p,k,ltisys)	*Creates a continuous-time zero-pole-gain model with zeros z, poles p and gains k with generic properties inherited from the LTI model ltisys.*
sys=zpk(z,p,k,p1,v1,p2,v2,...)	*Creates a continuous-time zero-pole-gain model with zeros z, poles p and gains k and properties given by the property/value pairs (pi, vi).*
sys=zpk(z,p,k,Ts,p1,v1,p2,v2,..)	*Creates a discrete-time zero-pole-gain model with zeros z, poles p, gains k and sample time Ts, and properties given by the property/value pairs (pi, vi).*
sys = zpk('s')	*Specifies a continuous-time zero-pole-gain model using a rational function in the Laplace variable s.*
sys = zpk('z',Ts)	*Specifies a discrete-time zero-pole-gain model using a rational function in the discrete-time variable z.*
zsys = zpk(sys)	*Converts an LTI model sys into a zero-pole-gain model.*
zsys = zpk(sys,'inv')	*Converts an LTI model sys into a zero-pole-gain model using investment formulas.*
[z,p,k] = zpkdata(sys)	*Returns the zeros z, poles p and gains k of the model sys.*
[z,p,k] = zpkdata(sys,'v')	*Returns the zeros z, poles p and gains k of the model sys as column vectors.*
[z,p,k,Ts,Td] = zpkdata(sys)	*Returns in addition to the above the sample time Ts and the input lag Td.*

As a first example, we generate a random discrete LTI system with three states, two inputs and two outputs.

```
>> sys = drss(3,2,2)
```

a =

	x1	x2	x3
x1	-0.048856	0.40398	0.23064
x2	0.068186	0.35404	-0.40811
x3	-0.46016	-0.089457	-0.036824

b =

	u1	u2
x1	-0.43256	0.28768
x2	0	-1.1465
x3	0.12533	1.1909

c =

	x1	x2	x3
y1	1.1892	0.32729	-0.18671
y2	-0.037633	0.17464	0.72579

d =

	u1	u2
y1	0	-0.1364
y2	2.1832	0

```
Sampling time: unspecified
Discrete-time model.
>>
```

In the following example, we create the model

$$5\frac{dx}{dt} = x + 2u$$

$$y = 3x + 4u$$

with a gap of 0.1 seconds and tagged as *'voltage'* entry.

```
>> sys = dss(1,2,3,4,5,0.1,'inputname','voltage')
a =
                          x1
          x1              1
b =
                       voltage
          x1              2
c =
                          x1
          y1              3

d =
                       voltage
          y1              4
e =
                          x1
          x1              5

Sampling time: 0.1
Discrete-time model.
```

The example below creates the following two-input digital filter:

$$H\left(z^{-1}\right) = \left[\frac{1}{1+z^{-1}+2z^{-2}} \quad \frac{1+0.3z^{-1}}{5+2z^{-1}}\right]$$

specifying time displays and channel entries *'channel1'* and *'channel2'* :

```
>> num = {1 , [1 0.3]}
den = {[1 1 2] ,[5 2]}
M = filt(num,den,'inputname',{'channel1' 'channel2'})

NUM =

[1.00] [double 1 x 2]
```

den =

[double 1 x 3]   [double 1 x 2]

Transfer function from input "channel1" to output:

$$\frac{1}{1 + z^{-1} + 2\ z^{-2}}$$

Transfer function from input "channel2" to output:

$$\frac{1 + 0.3\ z\ ^\wedge - 1}{5 + 2\ z\ ^\wedge - 1}$$

Sampling time: unspecified

Next we create a SISO FRD model.

```
>> freq = logspace(1,2);
resp = .05*(freq).*exp(i*2*freq);
sys = frd(resp,freq)
```

From input 1 to:

Frequency(rad/s)	output 1
10.000000	0.204041+0.456473i
10.481131	-0.270295+0.448972i
10.985411	-0.549157+0.011164i
11.513954	-0.293037-0.495537i
12.067926	0.327595-0.506724i
12.648552	0.623904+0.103480i
13.257114	0.124737+0.651013i
13.894955	-0.614812+0.323543i
14.563485	-0.479139-0.548328i
15.264180	0.481814-0.591898i
15.998587	0.668563+0.439215i
16.768329	-0.438184+0.714799i
17.575106	-0.728874-0.490870i
18.420700	0.602513-0.696623i
19.306977	0.588781+0.765007i
.	
.	
.	
86.851137	-2.649156-3.440897i
91.029818	4.498503-0.692487i
95.409548	-3.261293+3.481583i
100.000000	2.435938-4.366486i

Continuous-time frequency response data model.

Now we define an FRD model and its data is returned.

```
>> freq = logspace(1,2,2);
resp = .05*(freq).*exp(i*2*freq);
sys = frd(resp,freq);
[resp,freq] = frdata(sys,'v')

resp =
          0.20
          2.44
freq =
         10.00
        100.00
```

The following example creates a 2-output/1-input transfer function:

$$H(p) = \begin{bmatrix} \dfrac{p+1}{p^2+2p+2} \\ \dfrac{1}{p} \end{bmatrix}$$

```
>> num = {[1 1] ; 1}
den = {[1 2 2] ; [1 0]}
H = tf(num,den)

NUM =

[double 1 x 2]
[1.00]

den =

[double 1 x 3]
[1x2 double]
Transfer function from input to output...
          s + 1
#1:  -------------
     s ^ 2 + 2 s + 2


       1
#2:  -
       s
```

The following example computes the transfer function for the following state-space model:

$$A = \begin{bmatrix} -2 & -1 \\ 1 & -2 \end{bmatrix}, B = \begin{bmatrix} 1 & 1 \\ 2 & -1 \end{bmatrix}, C = \begin{bmatrix} 1 & 0 \end{bmatrix}, D = \begin{bmatrix} 0 & 1 \end{bmatrix}$$

```
>> sys = ss([-2 -1;1 -2],[1 1;2 -1],[1 0],[0 1])
tf(sys)
```

a =

	x1	x2
x1	-2	-1
x2	1	-2

b =

	u1	u2
x1	1	1
x2	2	-1

c =

	x1	x2
y1	1	0

d =

	u1	u2
y1	0	1

Continuous-time model.

Transfer function from input 1 to output:

```
s - 2.963e-016
--------------
s^2 + 4 s + 5
```

Transfer function from input 2 to output:

```
s ^ 2 + 5 s + 8
-------------
s ^ 2 + 4 s + 5
```

The following example specifies two discrete-time transfer functions:

$$g(z) = \frac{z+1}{z^2 + 2z + 3} \qquad h(z^{-1}) = \frac{1 + z^{-1}}{1 + 2z^{-1} + 3z^{-2}} = zg(z)$$

```
>> g = tf([1 1],[1 2 3],0.1)
```

Transfer function:

```
   z + 1
-------------
z^2 + 2 z + 3
```

Sampling time: 0.1

```
>> h = tf([1 1],[1 2 3],0.1,'variable','z^-1')
```

Transfer function:

```
      1 + z^-1
--------------------
1 + 2 z^-1 + 3 z^-2
```

Sampling time: 0.1

We now specify the zero-pole-gain model associated with the transfer function:

$$H(z) = \begin{bmatrix} \dfrac{1}{z-0.3} \\ \dfrac{2(z+0.5)}{(z-0.1+j)(z-0.1-j)} \end{bmatrix}$$

```
>> z = {[] ; -0.5}
p = {0.3 ; [0.1+i 0.1-i]}
k = [1 ; 2]
H = zpk(z,p,k,-1)

z =

[]
[-0.5000]

p =

[    0.3000]
[1x2 double]

k =

1
2

Zero/pole/gain from input to output...

          1
#1:   -------
       (z-0.3)

          2 (z+0.5)
#2:   -------------------
       (z^2 - 0.2z + 1.01)

Sampling time: unspecified
```

In the following example the transfer function tf([-10 20 0],[1 7 20 28 19 5]) is converted into zero-pole-gain format.

```
>> h = tf([-10 20 0],[1 7 20 28 19 5])
```

Transfer function:

```
           -10 s^2 + 20 s
-------------------------------------------
s^5 + 7 s^4 + 20 s^3 + 28 s^2 + 19s + 5
```

```
>> zpk(h)
```

Zero/pole/gain:

```
      -10 s (s-2)
----------------------
(s) ^ 3 (s ^ 2 + 4s + 5)
```

Model Feature Commands

Command	Description
str = class(object)	Displays a string describing which type of model object is ('tf', 'zpk', 'ss', or 'frd').
hasdelay(sys)	Returns 1 if the LTI model sys has input, output, input/output or internal delays, and returns 0 otherwise.
k= isa(obj,'class')	Returns 1 if the object is of the given class.
boo = isct(sys)	Returns 1 if the LTI model sys is continuous.
boo = isdt(sys)	Returns 1 if the LTI model sys is discrete.
boo = isempty(sys)	Returns 1 if the LTI model sys has no input or output.
boo = isproper(sys)	Returns 1 if the LTI model sys is proper.
boo = issiso(sys)	Returns 1 if the LTI model sys is SISO.
n = ndims(sys)	Returns the number of dimensions in the LTI model or model array sys.
size(sys)	Displays the number of inputs/outputs of sys.
d = size(sys)	Assigns the number of inputs/outputs of sys to d.
Ny = size(sys,1)	Returns the number of outputs of sys.
Nu = size(sys,2)	Returns the number of inputs of sys.
Sk = size(sys,2+k)	Returns the length of the k-th dimension of the array when sys is an LTI array.
Ns = size(sys,'order')	Returns the order of the (TS, SS, or ZPK) model sys.
Nf = size(sys,'frequency')	Returns the frequency of the FRD model sys.

Model Conversion Commands

Command	Description
sysd = c2d(sys,Ts)	Converts a continuous model sys to a discrete model sysd using zero-order hold on the inputs and a sample time of Ts seconds.
sysd = c2d(sys,Ts,method)	Converts a continuous model sys to a discrete model sysd using zero-order hold on the inputs and a sample time of Ts seconds using the specified method of discretization. The method can be zero-order hold (zoh), triangle approximation (foh), impulse invariant discretization (impulse), Bilinear (Tustin) (tustin) or zero-pole matching (matched).
[sysd, G] = c2d(sys,Ts,method)	In addition to the above, returns a matrix G that maps the continuous initial conditions x0 and u0 of the state-space model sys to the discrete-time initial state vector x[0]. The possible methods of discretization are descxribed above.
sys = chgFreqUnit(sys,units)	Changes units of the frequency points in sys to new units given by units.
sysc = d2c(sysd)	Converts a discrete model sysd to a continuous model sysc using zero-order hold on the inputs.
sysc = d2c(sysd,method)	Converts a discrete model sysd to a continuous model sysc using the conversion method given by method. The possible methods of conversion are zoh, foh, tustin and matched (see above).
sys1 = d2d(sys,Ts)	Resamples the discrete-time model sys to produce an equivalent discrete-time model sys1 with new sample time Ts.
sys = delay2z(sys)	Replaces delays of discrete-time TF, SS or ZPK models by poles at z=0, or replaces delays of FRD models by phase shift. [Note: more recent versions of MATLAB have replaced delay2z by absorbDelay.]
sys = frd(r,f)	Creates an FRD model sys from the frequency response data stored in the array r. The vector f represents the underlying frequencies for the frequency response data.
sys = frd(r,f,Ts)	Creates a discrete-time FRD model with sample time Ts in seconds.
sys = frd	Creates an empty FRD model.
sys = frd(r,f,ltisys)	Creates an FRD model which inherits the generic properties of the LTI model ltisys.
sysfrd = frd(sys,f)	Converts a TF, SS or ZPK model to an FRD model with frequencies f.
sysfrd = frd(sys,f,units)	Converts a TF, SS or ZPK model to an FRD model with frequencies f specifying the units ('rad/s' or 'Hz').

(continued)

Command	Description
[num, den] = pade(T,N)	*Returns the Padé approximation of order N of the continuous-time I/O delay exp(–sT) in transfer function form. The row vectors num and den contain the numerator and denominator coefficients in descending powers of s. Both are Nth-order polynomials.*
pade(T,N)	*Plots the step and phase responses of the Nth-order Padé approximation and compares them with the exact responses of the model with I/O delay T.*
sysx = pade(sys,N)	*Produces a delay-free approximation sysx of the continuous delay system sys. All delays are replaced by their Nth-order Padé approximation.*
sysx = pade(sys,Nu,Ny,NINT)	*Specifies independent approximation orders for each input, output, and I/O or internal delay. Here NU, NY and NINT are integer arrays: NU is the vector of approximation orders for the input channel; NY is the vector of approximation orders for the output channel; NINT is the approximation order for I/O delays (TF or ZPK models) or internal delays (state-space models).*
sys = reshape(sys,s1,s2,...,sk) **sys = reshape(sys,[s1s2... sk])**	*Reshapes the LTI model sys to an array of LTI models.*
[r, p, k] = residue(b,a)	*Finds the residues, poles, and direct term of a partial fraction expansion of the ratio of two polynomials, b(s) and a(s), where b and a are the vectors listing the numerator and denominator coefficients, respectively.*
[b,a] = residue(r,p,k)	*Converts the partial fraction expansion back to the polynomials with coefficients in b and a.*
sys = ss(A,B,C,D,E).	*Creates the continuous-time state-space model:* $$E\frac{dx}{dt} = Ax + Bu$$ $$y = Cx + Du$$
sys = ss(A,B,C,D,E,Ts)	*Creates the discrete-time state-space model (with sample time Ts in seconds):* $$Ex[n+1] = Ax[n]Bu[n]$$ $$y[n] = Cx[n] + Du[n]$$
sys = ss(A,B,C,D,E,ltisys)	*Creates a continuous-time state-space model with generic properties inherited from the LTI model ltisys.*
sys = ss(A,B,C,D,E,p1,p2,v1,v2,...)	*Creates a continuous-time state-space model with properties given by the property/value pairs (pi, vi).*
sys= ss(A,B,C,D,E,Ts,p1,v1,p2,v2,...)	*Creates a discrete-time state-space model with sample time Ts and properties given by the property/value pairs (pi, vi).*
sys_ss = ss(sys)	*Converts the (TF or ZPK) model sys to a state-space model.*
sys_ss = ss(sys,'minimal')	*Produces a state-space realization with no uncontrollable or unobservable states*
sys = tf(num,den)	*Creates a continuous-time transfer function with specified numerator and denominator.*
sys = tf(num,den,Ts)	*Creates a discrete-time transfer function with specified numerator and denominator and sample time of Ts seconds.*

(continued

Command	Description
sys = tf(M)	Creates a static gain M (matrix or scalar).
sys = tf(num,den,ltisys)	Creates a transfer function with specified numerator and denominator and generic properties inherited from the LTI model ltisys.
sys = tf(num,den,p1,v1,p2,v2,...)	Creates a continuous-time transfer function with specified numerator and denominator and with properties given by the property/value pairs (pi, vi).
sys = tf(num,den,Ts,p1,v1,p2,v2,...)	Creates a discrete-time transfer function with specified numerator and denominator, sample time Ts in seconds, and properties given by the property/value pairs (pi, vi).
s = tf('s')	Specifies a TF model using a rational function in the Laplace variable s.
z = tf('z',Ts)	Specifies a TF model with sample time Ts using a rational function in the discrete-time variable z.
tfsys = tf(sys)	Converts a (TF or ZPK) model sys to a transfer function.
tfsys = tf(sys,'inv')	Converts a (TF or ZPK) model sys to a transfer function using investment formulas.
sys = zpk(z,p,k)	Creates a continuous-time zero-pole-gain model with zeros z, poles p and gains k.
sys = zpk(z,p,k,Ts)	Creates a discrete-time zero-pole-gain model with zeros z, poles p, gains k and sample time Ts in seconds.
sys = zpk(M)	Specifies a static gain M.
sys = zpk(z,p,k,ltisys)	Creates a continuous-time zero-pole-gain model with zeros z, poles p and gains k with generic properties inherited from the LTI model ltisys.
sys = zpk(z,p,k,p1,v1,p2,v2,...)	Creates a continuous-time zero-pole-gain model with zeros z, poles p and gains k and properties given by the property/value pairs (pi, vi).
sys = zpk(z,p,k,Ts,p1,v1,p2,v2,..)	Creates a discrete-time zero-pole-gain model with zeros z, poles p, gains k and sample time Ts, and properties given by the property/value pairs (pi, vi).
sys = zpk('s')	Specifies a continuous-time zero-pole-gain model using a rational function in the Laplace variable s.
sys = zpk('z',Ts)	Specifies a discrete-time zero-pole-gain model using a rational function in the discrete-time variable z.
zsys = zpk(sys)	Converts an LTI model sys into a zero-pole-gain model.
zsys = zpk(sys,'inv')	Converts an LTI model sys into a zero-pole-gain model using investment formulas.

As a first example, we consider the system:

$$H(s) = \frac{s-1}{s^2 + 4s + 5}$$

with input lag $Td = 0.35$ seconds. The system is discretized using triangular approximation with sampling time $Ts = 0.1$ sec.

```
> H = tf([1 -1],[1 4 5],'inputdelay',0.35)
```

Transfer function:

$$exp(-0.35*s) * \frac{s - 1}{s^2 + 4s + 5}$$

```
>> Hd = c2d(H,0.1,'foh')
```

Transfer function:

$$z^{(-3)} * \frac{0.0115\ z^3 + 0.0456\ z^2 - 0.0562z - 0.009104}{z^3 - 1.629\ z^2 + 0.6703z}$$

Sampling time: 0.1

If we want to compare the step response and its discretization (see Figure 3-9) we can use the following command:

```
>> step(H,'-',Hd,'--')
```

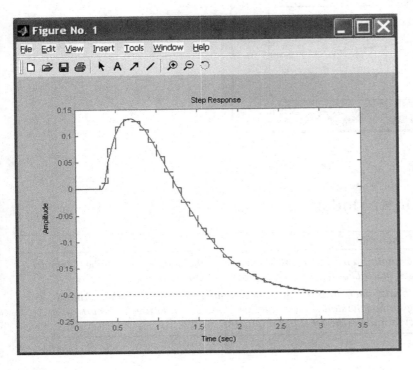

Figure 3-9.

The next example computes a Padé approximation of third order with I/O lag 0.1 seconds and compares the time and frequency response with its approximation (Figure 3-10).

```
>> pade(0.1,3)
Step response of 3rd-order Pade approximation
```

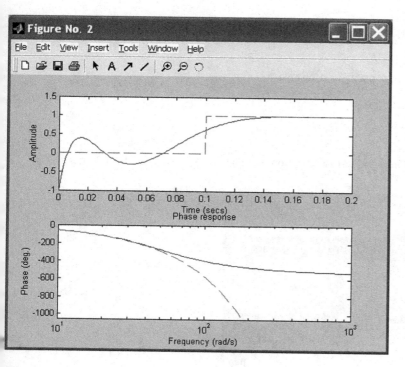

Figure 3-10.

Commands for Reduced Order Models

Command	Description
[sysb,g] = balreal(sys)	*Computes a balanced realization sysb for the stable portion of the LTI model sys. balreal handles both continuous and discrete systems.*
[sysb,g,T,Ti] = balreal(sys)	*In addition returns the vector g containing the diagonal of the balanced gramian, the state similarity transformation $x_b = Tx$ used to convert sys to sysb, and the inverse transformation $Ti = T^{-1}$*

(*continued*)

Command	Description
sysr = minreal(sys)	*Eliminates uncontrollable or unobservable states in state-space models, or cancels pole-zero pairs in transfer functions or zero-pole-gain models.*
sysr = minreal(sys,tol)	*Specifies the tolerance used for state elimination or pole-zero cancellation. The default value is tol = sqrt(eps) and increasing this tolerance forces additional cancellations.*
[sysr,u] = minreal(sys,tol)	*In addition finds an orthogonal matrix U such that (U*A*U',U*B,C*U') is a Kalman decomposition of (A,B,C).*
rsys = modred(sys,elim)	*Reduces the order of a continuous or discrete state-space model sys by eliminating the states found in the vector elim. The full state vector X is partitioned as X = [X1;X2] where X1 is the reduced state vector and X2 is discarded.*
rsys = modred(sys,elim,'method')	*In addition specifies the state elimination method, which can be MatchDC (enforce matching DC gains) or Truncate (delete X2).*
MSYS = sminreal(sys)	*Eliminates the states of the state-space model sys that don't affect the input/output response.*

In the example that follows we consider the zero-pole-gain model defined by *sys = zpk([- 10 - 20.01], [- 5 - 9.9 -20.1], 1)* and estimate a balanced realization, presenting the diagonal of the balanced grammian.

```
>> sys = zpk([-10 -20.01],[-5 -9.9 -20.1],1)
```

Zero/pole/gain:

```
   (s+10) (s+20.01)
----------------------
(s+5) (s+9.9) (s+20.1)
```

```
>> [sysb,g] = balreal(sys)
```

a =

	x1	*x2*	*x3*
x1	*-4.97*	*0.2399*	*0.2262*
x2	*-0.2399*	*-4.276*	*-9.467*
x3	*0.2262*	*9.467*	*-25.75*

b =

	u1
x1	*-1*
x2	*-0.02412*
x3	*0.02276*

c =

	x1	*x2*	*x3*
y1	*-1*	*0.02412*	*0.02276*

```
d =
          u1
   y1    0
```

Continuous-time model.

```
g =
    0.1006
    0.0001
    0.0000
```

The result shows that the last two states are weakly coupled to the input and output, so it will be convenient to remove them by using the syntax:

```
>> sysr = modred(sysb,[2 3],'del')
```

```
a =
          x1
   x1   -4.97
```

```
b =
         u1
   x1   -1
```

```
c =
         x1
   y1   -1
```

```
d =
         u1
   y1    0
```

Continuous-time model.

Now we can compare the answers of the original and reduced models (Figure 3-11) by using the following syntax:

```
>> bode(sys,'-',sysr,'x')
```

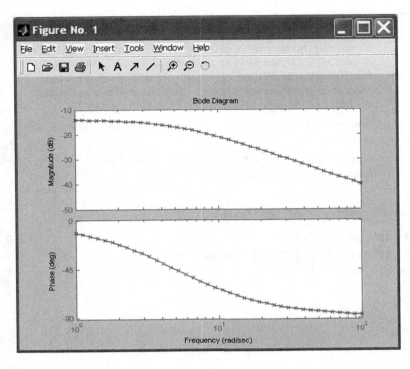

Figure 3-11.

Commands Related to State-Spaces

Command	Description
csys = canon(sys,'type')	*Transforms the linear model sys into a canonical state-space model csys. The argument 'type' can be either 'modal' or 'companion.'*
[csys,T] = canon(sys,'type')	*In addition returns the state-coordinate transformation T that relates the states of the state-space model sys to the states of csys.*
Co = ctrb(A,B) **Co = ctrb(sys)**	*Returns the controllability matrix for state-space systems.*
[Abar,Bbar,Cbar,T,k] = ctrbf(A,B,C) **[Abar,Bbar,Cbar,T,k] = ctrbf(A,B,C,tol)**	*Decomposes the state-space system represented by A, B, and C into the controllability staircase form, Abar, Bbar, and Cbar. T is the similarity transformation matrix and k is a vector of length n, where n is the order of the system represented by A. The number of non-null values of k indicates the number of iterations needed to calculate T.*
Wc = gram(sys,'c') **Wo = gram(sys,'o')**	*Calculates the controllability and observability grammians of the state-space model sys.*
Ob = obsv(A,B) **Ob = obsv(sys)**	*Calculates the observability matrix for state-space models.*

(*continued*

Command	Description
[Abar,Bbar,Cbar,T,k] = obsvf(A,B,C) [Abar,Bbar,Cbar,T,k] = obsvf(A,B,C,tol)	*Decomposes the state-space system with matrices A, B, and C into the observability staircase form Abar, Bbar, and Cbar. T is the similarity transformation matrix and k is a vector of length n, where n is the order of the system represented by A. The number of non-null values of k indicates the number of iterations needed to calculate T.*
sysT = ss2ss(sys,T)	*Returns the transformed state-space model sysT given sys and the state coordinate transformation T.*
[sysb,T] = ssbal(sys) [sysb,T] = ssbal(sys,condT)	*Balances state-space models using a diagonal similarity transformation.*

As a first example we consider the following continuous state-space model:

$$A = \begin{bmatrix} 1 & 10^4 & 10^2 \\ 0 & 10^2 & 10^5 \\ 10 & 1 & 0 \end{bmatrix}, \ B = \begin{bmatrix} 1 \\ 1 \\ 1 \end{bmatrix}, \ C = \begin{bmatrix} 0.1 & 10 & 100 \end{bmatrix}$$

We calculate the balanced model as follows:

```
>> a = [1 1e4 1e2; 0 1e2 1e5; 10 1 0];
b = [1; 1; 1];
c = [0.1 10 1e2];
sys ss (a, b, c, 0) =

a =
          x1       x2      x3
    x1     1    1e+004     100
    x2     0       100   1e+005
    x3    10         1       0

b =
         u1
    x1    1
    x2    1
    x3    1

c =
         x1    x2    x3
    y1   0.1   10   100

d =
         u1
    y1    0

Continuous-time model.
```

In the following example we calculate the observability matrix of the ladder system
$A = [1, 1; 4, -2]$, $B = [1, -1, 1, -1]$, $C = [0, 1; 1, 0]$

```
>> A = [1, 1; 4, - 2]; B = [1, - 1, 1, - 1]; C = [1,0; 0.1];
>> [Abar, Bbar, Cbar, T, k] = obsvf(A,B,C)

Abar =

    1    1
    4   -2

Bbar =

    1   -1
    1   -1

Cbar =

    1    0
    0    1

T =

    1    0
    0    1

k =

    2    0
```

Below we calculate the controllability matrix of the system in the previous example.

```
>> A = [1, 1; 4, - 2]; B = [1, - 1, 1, - 1]; C = [1,0; 0.1];
>> [Abar, Bbar, Cbar, T, k] = ctrbf(A,B,C)

Abar =

   -3.0000    0.0000
    3.0000    2.0000

Bbar =

         0         0
   -1.4142    1.4142

Cbar =

   -0.7071   -0.7071
    0.7071   -0.7071
```

$T =$

```
    -0.7071     0.7071
    -0.7071    -0.7071
```

$k =$

```
    1        0
```

Commands for Dynamic Models

Command	Description
[Wn,Z] = damp(sys) [Wn,Z,P] = damp(sys)	Displays a table of the damping ratio, natural frequency, and time constant of the poles of the linear model sys. You can also get the vector P of the poles of sys.
k = dcgain(sys)	Calculates the low-frequency (DC) gain of the model sys.
[P,Q] = covar(sys,W)	Calculates the stationary covariance of the output of an LTI model sys driven by Gaussian white noise inputs W. P is the steady-state output response covariance and Q is the steady-state state covariance.
s = dsort(p) [s,ndx] = dsort(p)	Sorts the discrete-time poles contained in the vector p in descending order by magnitude.
s = esort(p) [s,ndx] = esort(p)	Sorts the continuous-time poles contained in the vector p by real part.
norm(sys)	Calculates the H^2 norm of the model sys.
norm(sys,2)	Calculates the H^2 norm of the model sys.
norm(sys,inf)	Calculates the H_∞ norm of the model sys.
norm(sys,inf,tol)	Calculates the H_∞ norm of the model sys with tolerance tol.
[ninf,fpeak] = norm(sys)	Calculates, in addition to the H_∞ norm, the frequency fpeak at which the gain reaches its peak value.
p = pole(sys)	Calculates the poles of the LTI model sys.
d = eig(A)	Returns the vector of eigenvalues of A.
d = eig(A,B)	Returns the generalized eigenvalues of the pair(A,B).
[V,D] = eig(A)	Returns the eigenvalues and eigenvectors of the matrix A.
[V,D] = eig(A,'nobalance')	Returns the eigenvalues and eigenvectors of A without a preliminary balancing step.
[V,D] = eig(A,B)	Returns the eigenvalues and generalized eigenvectors of (A,B).
[V,D] = eig(A,B,flag)	Returns the eigenvalues and generalized eigenvectors of (A,B). The factorization method ('chol' or 'qz') is specified by flag.
pzmap(sys) pzmap(sys1,sys2,...,sysN) [p,z] = pzmap(sys)	Creates a pole-zero plot of the continuous-time or discrete-time dynamic system sys or of several LTI systems sys1, sys2,..., sysn at the same time. [p, z] gives the poles and zeros and not the graph.

(continued)

Command	Description
rlocus(sys)	*Calculates and plots the root locus of the open-loop SISO model sys.*
rlocus(sys,k)	*Uses the user-specified vector k of gains to plot the root locus.*
rlocus(sys1,sys2,...)	*Calculates and plots the root locus of several systems in a simple graph.*
[r,k] = rlocus(sys)	*Returns the vector k of selected gains and the complex root locations r for these gains.*
r = rlocus(sys,k)	*Returns the root locations r for a system sys with selected gains given by the vector k.*
r = roots(c)	*Returns the roots of the polynomial c as a column vector.*
sgrid	*Generates, for pole-zero and root locus plots, a grid of constant damping factors from zero to one in steps of 0.1 and natural frequencies from zero to 10 rad/sec in steps of one rad/sec, and plots the grid over the current axis.*
zgrid	*Similarly generates a grid from zero to π in steps of π/10, and plots the grid over the current axis.*
z = zero(sys)	*Calculates the zeros of the LTI model sys.*
[z,gain] = zero(sys)	*Returns the zeros and gain of the LTI system sys.*

As a first example, we calculate the eigenvalues, natural frequencies and damping factors of the continuous transfer function model:

$$H(s) = \frac{2s^2 + 5s + 1}{s^2 + 2s + 3}$$

```
>> H = tf([2 5 1],[1 2 3])
```

Transfer function:

```
2 s^2 + 5 s + 1
---------------
s^2 + 2 s + 3
```

```
>> damp(H)
```

Eigenvalue   Damping   Freq. (rad/s)

```
00e - 1 + 000 + 1. 41e + 000i 5. 77e-001 1. 73e + 000
00e - 1 + 000 - 1. 41e + 000i 5. 77e-001 1. 73e + 000
```

In the following example we calculate the DC gain of the MIMO transfer function model:

$$H(s) = \begin{bmatrix} 1 & \dfrac{s-1}{s^2+s+3} \\ \dfrac{1}{s+1} & \dfrac{s+2}{s-3} \end{bmatrix}$$

```
>> H = [1 tf([1 -1],[1 1 3]) ; tf(1,[1 1]) tf([1 2],[1 -3])]
dcgain(H)
```

Transfer function from input 1 to output...

#1:   1

```
          1
#2:    -----
       s + 1
```

Transfer function from input 2 to output...

```
            s
#1:    -----------
       s^2 + s + 3
```

```
       s + 2
#2:    -----
        3s
```

ans =

```
1.0000 - 0.3333
1.0000 - 0.6667
```

Next we consider the discrete-time transfer function

$$H(z) = \frac{z^3 - 2.841z^2 + 2.875z - 1.004}{z^3 - 2.417z^2 + 2.003z - 0.5488}$$

with 0.1 second sampling time and calculate the 2-norm and the infinite norm with its optimum value.

```
>> H = tf([1 -2.841 2.875 -1.004],[1 -2.417 2.003 -0.5488],0.1)
norm(H)
```

Transfer function:

```
z^3 - 2.841 z^2 + 2.875 z - 1.004
---------------------------------
z^3 - 2.417 z^2 + 2.003 z - 0.5488
```

Sampling time: 0.1

ans =

1.2438

```
>> [ninf,fpeak] = norm(H,inf)
```

surrounded =

2.5488

fpeak =

3.0844

We then confirm the previous values by generating the Bode plot of *H(z)* (see Figure 3-12).

```
>> bode (H)
```

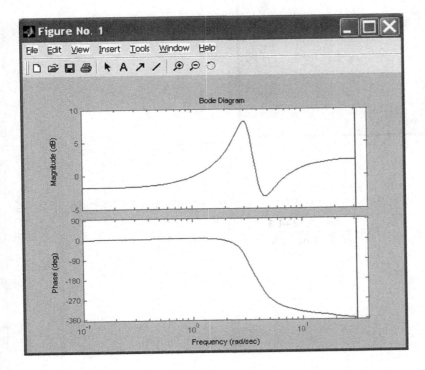

Figure 3-12.

Next we calculate and graph the root locus of the following system (see Figure 3-13):

$$h(s) = \frac{2s^2 + 5s + 1}{s^2 + 2s + 3}$$

```
>> h = tf([2 5 1],[1 2 3]);
rlocus (h)
```

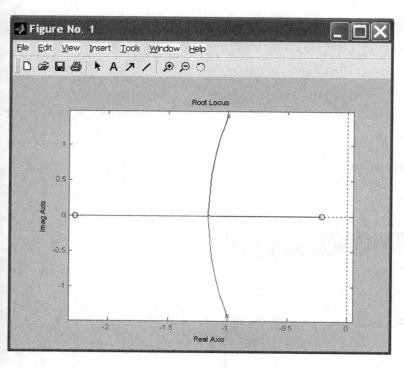

Figure 3-13.

In the example below we plot a *z*-plane grid over the root locus of the following system (see Figure 3-14):

$$H(z) = \frac{2z^2 - 3.4z + 1.5}{z^2 - 1.6z + 0.8}$$

```
> H = tf([2 -3.4 1.5],[1 -1.6 0.8],-1)

Transfer function:

2 z^2 - 3.4 z + 1.5
-------------------
z^2 - 1.6 z + 0.8

Sampling time: unspecified

>> rlocus(H)
zgrid
axis('square')
```

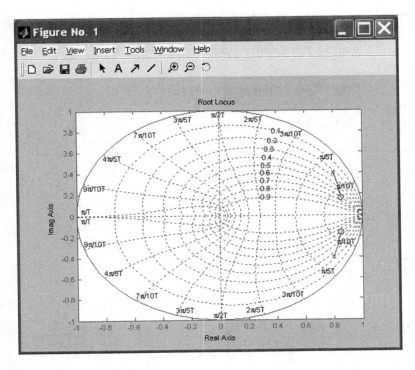

Figure 3-14.

Commands for Interconnecting Models

Command	Description
sys = append(sys1,sys2,...,sysN)	*Combines models in a diagonal configuration block. Groups the models together by appending their inputs and outputs (Figure 3-15).*
asys = augstate (sys)	*Appends the state vector to the output vector.*
sysc = connect(sys,Q,inputs,outputs)	*Connects the subsystems in a block according to a chosen interconnection scheme (given by the connection matrix Q).*
sys = feedback(sys1,sys2) sys = feedback(sys1,sys2,sign) sys = feedback(sys1,sys2,feedin,feedout,sign)	*Returns a model sys for the negative feedback interconnection of models sys1 and sys2 (see Figure 3-16). May include sign and closed loop (see Figure 3-17).*
sys = lft(sys1,sys2) sys = lft(sys1,sys2,nu,ny)	*Forms the linear fractional transformation (LFT) of two models (see Figure 3-18).*
[A,B,C,D] = ord2(wn,z) [num,den] = ord2(wn,z)	*Generates continuous second-order systems (wn is the natural frequency and z is the damping factor).*

(*continued*

Command	Description
sys = parallel(sys1,sys2)	*Connects two systems in parallel (see Figure 3-19).*
sys = parallel(sys1,sys2,inp1,inp2,out1,out2)	
sys = series(sys1,sys2)	*Connects two systems in series (see Figure 3-20).*
sys = series(sys1,sys2,outputs1,inputs2)	
sys = stack(arraydim,sys1,sys2,...)	*Produces an array of dynamic system models by stacking the models sys1,sys2,... along the array dimension arraydim.*

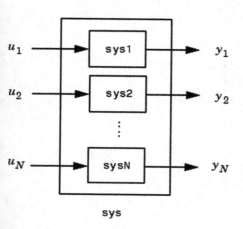

Figure 3-15.

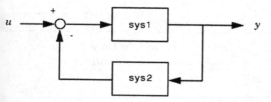

Figure 3-16.

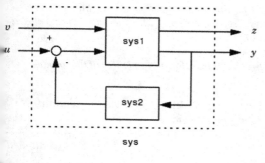

Figure 3-17.

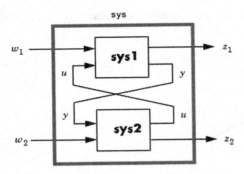

Figure 3-18.

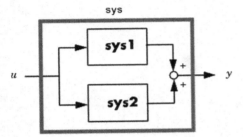

Figure 3-19.

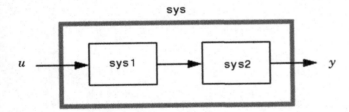

Figure 3-20.

As a first example we will combine the systems $tf(1, [1\ 0])$ and $ss(1,2,3,4)$. We should bear in mind that for systems with transfer functions $H_1(s), H_2(s), ..., H_n(s)$, the resulting combined system has as transfer function:

$$\begin{bmatrix} H_1(s) & 0 & ... & 0 \\ 0 & H_2(s) & ... & ... \\ ... & ... & ... & 0 \\ 0 & ... & 0 & H_n(s) \end{bmatrix}$$

For two systems *sys1* and *sys2* defined by (A_1, B_1, C_1, D_1) and (A_2, B_2, C_2, D_2), their combination *append*(*sys1, sys2*) yields the system:

$$\begin{bmatrix} \dot{x}_1 \\ \dot{x}_2 \end{bmatrix} = \begin{bmatrix} A_1 & 0 \\ 0 & A_2 \end{bmatrix} \begin{bmatrix} x_1 \\ x_2 \end{bmatrix} + \begin{bmatrix} B_1 & 0 \\ 0 & B_2 \end{bmatrix} \begin{bmatrix} u_1 \\ u_2 \end{bmatrix}$$

$$\begin{bmatrix} y_1 \\ y_2 \end{bmatrix} = \begin{bmatrix} C_1 & 0 \\ 0 & C_2 \end{bmatrix} \begin{bmatrix} x_1 \\ x_2 \end{bmatrix} + \begin{bmatrix} D_1 & 0 \\ 0 & D_2 \end{bmatrix} \begin{bmatrix} u_1 \\ u_2 \end{bmatrix}$$

For our example we have:

```
>> sys1 = tf(1,[1 0])
sys2 = ss(1,2,3,4)
sys = append(sys1,10,sys2)
```

Transfer function:

```
1
-
s

a =
        x1
   x1   1

b =
        u1
   x1   2

c =
        x1
   y1   3

d =
        u1
   y1   4
```

Continuous-time model.

```
a =
        x1   x2
   x1   0    0
   x2   0    1

b =
        u1   u2   u3
   x1   1    0    0
   x2   0    0    2
```

```
c =
        x1  x2
    y1   1   0
    y2   0   0
    y3   0   3

d =
        u1  u2  u3
    y1   0   0   0
    y2   0  10   0
    y3   0   0   4
```

Continuous-time model.

The following example, illustrated in Figure 3-21, attaches the plant $G(s)$ to the driver $H(s)$, defined below, using negative feedback:

$$G(s) = \frac{2s^2 + 5s + 1}{s^2 + 2s + 3}$$

$$H(s) = \frac{5(s+1)}{s+10}$$

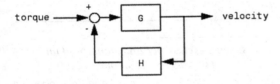

Figure 3-21.

```
>> G = tf([2 5 1],[1 2 3],'inputname','torque',...)
'outputname','velocity');
H = zpk(-2,-10,5)
Cloop = feedback(G,H)
```

Zero/pole/gain:

```
5 (s+2)
-------
(s+10)
```

Zero/pole/gain from input "torque" to output "velocity":

```
0.18182 (s+10) (s+2. 281) (s+0. 2192)
----------------------------------
(s+3. 419) (s ^ 2 + 1. 763s + 1.064)
```

The following example builds a second-order transfer function with damping factor 0.4 and natural frequency 2.4 rad/sec.

```
>> [num,den] = ord2(2.4,0.4)

num =

1

den =

1.0000    1.9200    5.7600

>> sys = tf(num,den)

Transfer function:

         1
-------------------
s ^ 2 + 1.92 s + 5.76
```

Response Time Commands

Command	Description
[u, t] = gensig(*type*,tau)	Generates a scalar signal u of class type and with period tau (in seconds). The type can be sine, square or pulse.
[u, t] = gensig(*type*,tau,Tf,Ts)	Also specifies the time duration Tf of the signal and the spacing Ts between the time samples t.
impulse(sys)	Calculates and plots the impulse response of the model sys.
impulse(sys,t)	Uses the user-supplied time vector t for simulation.
impulse(sys1,sys2,...,sysN)	Calculates and plots the impulse response of several models.
impulse(sys1,sys2,...,sysN,t)	Calculates and plots the impulse response of several models using the user-supplied time vector t for simulation.
impulse(sys1,'PlotStyle1',...,sysN,'PlotStyleN')	In addition sets graphics styles.
[y, t, x] = impulse(sys)	Returns the length of t, the number of outputs and the number of inputs for the impulse response of the model sys.
initial(sys,x0)	Calculates and plots the unforced response of the state-space model sys, or of several models, with initial condition x0. A user-supplied time vector t can be supplied as well as specified graphics styles. You can also obtain the length of t, the number of outputs and the number of inputs for the unforced response of the model sys.
initial(sys,x0,t)	
initial(sys1,sys2,...,sysN,x0)	
initial(sys1,sys2,...,sysN,x0,t)	
initial(sys1,'PlotStyle1',...,sysN,'PlotStyleN',x0)	
[y, t, x] = initial(sys,x0)	

(continued)

Command	Description
lsim(sys,u,t) **lsim(sys,u,t,x0)** **lsim(sys,u,t,x0,'zoh')** **lsim(sys,u,t,x0,'foh')** **lsim(sys1,sys2,...,sysN,u,t)** **lsim(sys1,sys2,...,sysN,u,t,x0)** **lsim(sys1,'PlotStyle1',...,sysN,'PlotStyleN',u,t)** **[y, t, x] = lsim(sys,u,t,x0)**	*Calculates and plots the time response of the state-space model sys, or of several models, with initial condition x0. A user-supplied time sample t can be supplied as well as specified graphics styles. The options zoh and foh specify how the input values should be interpolated between samples (zero-order hold or linear interpolation, respectively). You can also obtain the output response y, the time vector t used for simulation, and the state trajectories x.*
step(sys) **step(sys,t)** **step(sys1,sys2,...,sysN)** **step(sys1,sys2,...,sysN,t)** **step(sys1,'PlotStyle1',...,sysN,'PlotStyleN')** **[y, t, x] = step(sys)**	*Calculates and plots the step response of the LTI model sys, or several models. A user-supplied time sample t can be supplied as well as specified graphics styles. You can also obtain the output response y, the time vector t used for simulation, and the state trajectories x.*
ltiview **ltiview(sys1,sys2,...,sysn)** **ltiview('plottype',sys1,sys2,...,sysn)** **ltiview('plottype',sys,extras)** **ltiview('clear',viewers)** **ltiview('current'sys1,sys2,...,** **sysn,viewers)**	*Opens an LTI Viewer for LTI system response analysis for one or more systems and with different graphics options defined by plottype ('step,' 'impulse,' 'initial,' 'lsim,' 'pzmap' 'bode,' 'nyquist,' 'nichols' and 'sigma').*

As a first example we generate and plot a square signal with period 5 seconds, duration 30 seconds and sampling every 0.1 seconds (see Figure 3-22).

```
>> [u,t] = gensig('square',5,30,0.1);
>> plot(t,u)
axis([0 30-1 2])
```

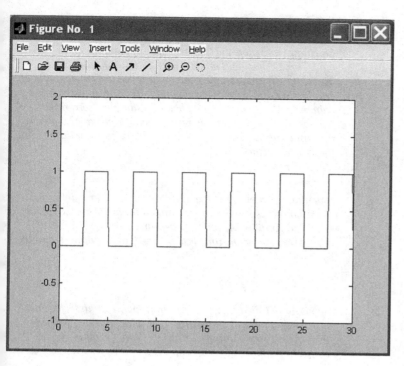

Figure 3-22.

In the example below we generate the response plot for the following state-space model (see Figure 3-23):

$$\begin{bmatrix} \dot{x}_1 \\ \dot{x}_2 \end{bmatrix} = \begin{bmatrix} -0.5572 & -0.7814 \\ 0.7814 & 0 \end{bmatrix} \begin{bmatrix} x_1 \\ x_2 \end{bmatrix}$$

$$y = \begin{bmatrix} 1.9691 & 6.4493 \end{bmatrix} \begin{bmatrix} x_1 \\ x_2 \end{bmatrix}$$

with initial conditions

$$x(0) = \begin{bmatrix} 1 \\ 0 \end{bmatrix}$$

```
>> a = [-0.5572   -0.7814;0.7814   0];
c = [1.9691   6.4493];
x0 = [1 ; 0]
sys = ss(a,[],c,[]);
initial (sys, x 0)

x 0 =

1
0
```

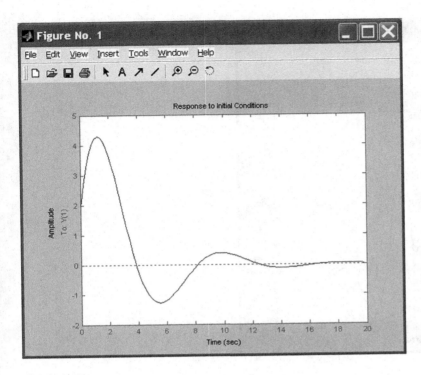

Figure 3-23.

Below we generate the step response plot of the following second order state-space model (see Figure 3-24):

$$\begin{bmatrix} \dot{x}_1 \\ \dot{x}_2 \end{bmatrix} = \begin{bmatrix} -0.5572 & -0.7814 \\ 0.7814 & 0 \end{bmatrix} \begin{bmatrix} x_1 \\ x_2 \end{bmatrix} + \begin{bmatrix} 1 & -1 \\ 0 & 2 \end{bmatrix} \begin{bmatrix} u_1 \\ u_2 \end{bmatrix}$$

$$y = \begin{bmatrix} 1.9691 & 6.4493 \end{bmatrix} \begin{bmatrix} x_1 \\ x_2 \end{bmatrix}$$

The following syntax is used:

```
>> a = [-0.5572    -0.7814;0.7814  0];
b = [1 -1;0 2];
c = [1.9691  6.4493];
sys = ss(a,b,c,0);
step(sys)
```

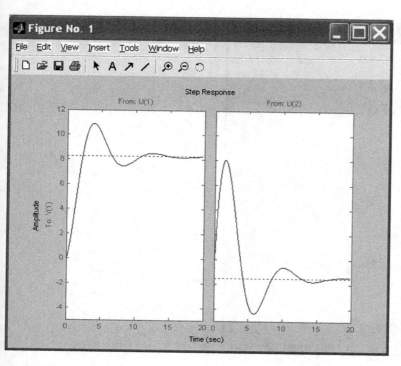

Figure 3-24.

Frequency Response Commands

Command	Description
S = allmargin(sys)	Computes the gain margin, phase margin, delay margin and the corresponding crossover frequencies of the SISO open-loop model sys.
bode(sys) bode(sys,w) bode(sys1,sys2,...,sysN) bode(sys1,sys2,...,sysN,w) bode(sys1,'PlotStyle1',..., sysN,'PlotStyleN') [mag,phase,w] = bode(sys)	Creates a Bode plot of the frequency response of the model sys, or of several systems. The frequency range can be specified by w as well as various graphics options. You can also obtain the magnitude, phase and frequency values of bode(sys).

(continued)

Command	Description
bodemag(sys) bodemag(sys,{wmin,wmax}) bodemag(sys,w) bodemag(sys1,sys2,...,sysN,w) bodemag(sys1,'PlotStyle1',..., sysN,'PlotStyleN')	Creates a Bode plot of the frequency response of the model sys, or of several models, without the phase diagram. The frequency range and various graphics options can be user-specified.
frsp = evalfr(sys,f)	Evaluates the transfer function of the system sys at the complex frequency f.
H = freqresp(sys,w)	Returns the frequency response of sys on the real frequency grid specified by the vector w.
isys = interp(sys,freqs)	Interpolates the frequency response data contained in the FRD model sys at the frequencies freqs.
y = linspace(a,b) y = linspace(a,b,n)	Creates a vector with 100 or n values equally spaced between a and b.
y = logspace(a,b) y = logspace(a,b,n) y = logspace(a,pi,n)	Creates a vector with uniform logarithmic spacing between 10^a and 10^b (50 points between 10^a and 10^b, n points between 10^a and 10^b or n points between 10^a and π).
[Gm,Pm,Wgm,Wpm] = margin(sys) [Gm,Pm,Wgm,Wpm] = margin(mag,phase,w) margin(sys)	Calculates the minimum gain margin, Gm, phase margin, Pm, and associated frequencies Wgm and Wpm of SISO open-loop models. Magnitude, phase and frequency vectors can be specified, and the Bode plot can be generated.
ngrid	Superimposes Nichols chart grid lines over the Nichols frequency response of a system.
nichols(sys) nichols(sys,w) nichols(sys1,sys2,...,sysN) nichols(sys1,sys2,...,sysN,w) nichols(sys1,'PlotStyle1',..., sysN,'PlotStyleN') [mag,phase,w] = nichols(sys) [mag,phase] = nichols(sys,w)	Creates a Nichols chart of the frequency response of a model. The arguments have the same meanings as for the Bode plot.

(continued)

Command	Description
nyquist(sys)	Creates a Nyquist plot of the frequency response of a model. The arguments have the same meanings as for the Bode plot.
nyquist(sys,w)	
nyquist(sys1,sys2,...,sysN)	
nyquist(sys1,sys2,...,sysN,w)	
nyquist(sys1,'PlotStyle1',...,	
sysN,'PlotStyleN')	
[re,im,w] = nyquist(sys)	
[re,im] = nyquist(sys,w)	
sigma(sys)	Calculates the singular values of the frequency response of a model.
sigma(sys,w)	
sigma(sys,w,type)	
sigma(sys1,sys2,...,sysN)	
sigma(sys1,sys2,...,sysN,w)	
sigma(sys1,sys2,...,sysN,w,type)	
sigma(sys1,'PlotStyle1',...,	
sysN,'PlotStyleN')	
[sv,w] = sigma(sys)	
sv = sigma(sys,w)	

As a first example we generate the Bode plot for the following continuous SISO system (see Figure 3-25):

$$H(s) = \frac{s^2 + 0.1s + 7.5}{s^4 + 0.12s^3 + 9s^2}$$

```
>> g = tf([1 0.1 7.5],[1 0.12 9 0 0]);
bode (g)
```

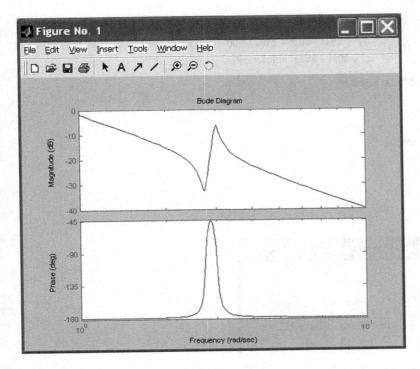

Figure 3-25.

Next we evaluate the following discrete-time transfer function at $z = 1 + i$:

$$H(z) = \frac{z-1}{z^2 + z + 1}$$

```
>> H = tf([1 -1],[1 1 1],-1)
z = 1+j
evalfr(H,z)
```

Transfer function:

```
   z - 1
-----------
z^2 + z + 1
```

Sampling time: unspecified

z =

1.0000 + 1. 0000i

ans =

0.2308 + 0. 1538i

Next we generate the Nichols chart, with grid, for the following system (see Figure 3-26):

$$H(s) = \frac{-4s^4 + 48s^3 - 18s^2 + 250s + 600}{s^4 + 30s^3 + 282s^2 + 525s + 60}$$

```
>> H = tf([-4 48 -18 250 600],[1 30 282 525 60])
```

Transfer function:

```
-4 s^4 + 48 s^3 - 18 s^2 + 250s + 600
---------------------------------------
s^4 + 30 s^3 + 282 s^2 + 525s + 60
```

```
>> nichols(H)
>> ngrid
```

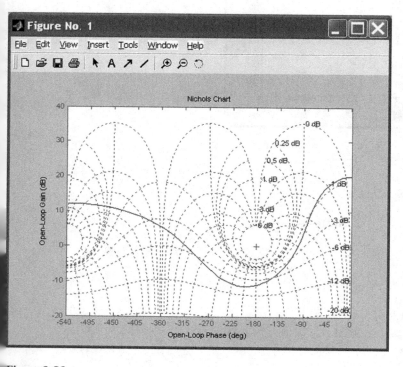

Figure 3-26.

Pole Location Commands

Command	Description
k = acker(A,b,p)	Given the single input system $$\frac{dx}{dt} = Ax + bu$$ and a vector p of desired closed-loop pole locations, using Ackermann's method, k is determined such that the eigenvalues of $A - bk$ match the entries of p (up to ordering).
K = place(A,B,p)	Given the single or multi-input system $$\frac{dx}{dt} = Ax + Bu$$ and a vector p of desired closed-loop pole locations, k is determined such that the eigenvalues of $A - bk$ match the entries of p (up to ordering).
est = estim(sys,L) est = estim(sys,L,sensors,known)	Produces a state/output estimator est given the plant state-space model sys and the estimator gain L. The measured outputs (sensors) and the known inputs (known) can be specified.
rsys = reg(sys,K,L) rsys = reg(sys,K,L,sensors,known,controls)	Forms a dynamic regulator or compensator rsys given a state-space model sys of the plant, a state-feedback gain matrix K, and an estimator gain matrix L. The measured outputs (sensors) and the known inputs (known) can be specified.

LQG Design Commands

Command	Description
[K, S, e] = lqr(A,B,Q,R) [K, S, e] = lqr(A,B,Q,R,N)	Calculates the LQ-optimal gain for continuous models.
[K, S, e] = dlqr(a,b,Q,R) [K, S, e] = dlqr(a,b,Q,R,N)	Calculates the LQ-optimal gain for discrete models.
[K,S,e] = lqry(sys,Q,R) [K,S,e] = lqry(sys,Q,R,N)	Calculates the LQ-optimum gain with weighted output.
[Kd,S,e] = lqrd(A,B,Q,R,Ts) [Kd,S,e] = lqrd(A,B,Q,R,N,Ts)	Calculates the discrete LQ gain for continuous models.
[kest,L,P] = kalman(sys,Qn,Rn,Nn) [kest,L,P,M,Z] = kalman(sys,Qn,Rn,Nn)	Computes the Kalman estimator for continuous and discrete models.
[kest,L,P,M,Z] = kalmd(sys,Qn,Rn,Ts)	Computes the discrete Kalman estimator for continuous models.
rlqg = lqgreg(kest,k) rlqg = lqgreg(kest,k,controls)	Forms the linear-quadratic-Gaussian (LQG) regulator by connecting the Kalman estimator designed with kalman and the optimal state-feedback gain designed with lqr, dlqr or lqry.

Commands for Solving Equations

Command	Description
[X,L,G,rr] = care(A,B,Q)	*Solves algebraic Riccati equations in continuous time.*
[X,L,G,rr] = care(A,B,Q,R,S,E)	
[X,L,G,report] = care(A,B,Q,...,'report')	
[X1,X2,L,report] = care(A,B,Q,...,'implicit')	
[X,L,G,rr] = dare(A,B,Q,R)	*Solves algebraic Riccati equations in discrete time.*
[X,L,G,rr] = dare(A,B,Q,R,S,E)	
[X,L,G,report] = dare(A,B,Q,...,'report')	
[X1,X2,L,report] = dare(A,B,Q,...,'implicit')	
X = lyap(A,Q)	*Solves continuous-time Lyapunov equations.*
X = lyap(A,B,C)	
X = dlyap(A,Q)	*Solves discrete-time Lyapunov equations.*

As an example, we solve the Riccati equation:

$$A^T X + XA - XBR^{-1}B^T X + C^T C = 0$$

where:

$$A = \begin{bmatrix} -3 & 2 \\ 1 & 1 \end{bmatrix} \quad B = \begin{bmatrix} 0 \\ 1 \end{bmatrix} \quad C = \begin{bmatrix} 1 & -1 \end{bmatrix} \quad R = 3$$

```
>> a = [-3 2;1 1]; b = [0 ; 1]; c = [1 -1]; r = 3;
[x,l,g] = care(a,b,c'*c,r)

x =

0.5895 1.8216
1.8216 8.8188

l =

-3.5026
-1.4370

g =

0.6072 2.9396
```

EXERCISE 3-1

Create the continuous state-space model and compute the realization of the state-space for the transfer function $H(s)$ defined below. Also find a minimal realization of $H(s)$.

$$H(s) = \begin{bmatrix} \dfrac{s+1}{s^3 + 3s^2 + 3s + 2} \\ \dfrac{s^2 + 3}{s^2 + s + 1} \end{bmatrix}$$

```
>> H = [tf([1 1],[1 3 3 2]) ; tf([1 0 3],[1 1 1])];
>> sys = ss(H)
```

```
a =
        x1      x2      x3      x4      x5
  x1    -3      -1.5    -1      0       0
  x2    2       0       0       0       0
  x3    0       1       0       0       0
  x4    0       0       0       -1      -0.5
  x5    0       0       0       2       0

b =
        U1
  x1    1
  x2    0
  x3    0
  x4    1
  x5    0

c =
        x1      x2      x3      x4      x5
  y1    0       0.5     0.5     0       0
  y2    0       0       0       -1      1

d =
        U1
  y1    0
  y2    1

Continuous-time model.
```

```
>> size(sys)
```

State-space model with 2 outputs, 1 input, and 5 states.

We have obtained a state-space model with 2 outputs, 1 input and 5 states. A minimal realization of $H(s)$ is found by using the syntax:

```
>> sys = ss(H,'min')
```

```
a =

            x1          x2          x3
   x1    -1.4183     -1.5188     0.21961
   x2    -0.14192    -1.7933     -0.70974
   x3    -0.44853     1.7658     0.21165

b =

            u1
   x1     0.19787
   x2     1.4001
   x3     0.02171

c =

            x1          x2          x3
   y1    -0.15944    0.018224    0.27783
   y2     0.35997    -0.77729    0.78688

d =

            u1
   y1        0
   y2        1

Continuous-time model.
```

```
>> size(sys)
```

```
State-space model with 2 outputs, 1 input, and 3 states.
```

A minimal realization is given by a state-space model with 2 outputs, 1 input and 3 states.

This result is in accordance with the following factorization of $H(s)$ as the composite of a first order system with a second order system:

$$H(s) = \begin{bmatrix} \dfrac{1}{s+2} & 0 \\ 0 & 1 \end{bmatrix} \begin{bmatrix} \dfrac{s+1}{s^2+s+1} \\ \dfrac{s^2+3}{s^2+s+1} \end{bmatrix}$$

EXERCISE 3-2

Find the discrete transfer function of the MIMO system $H(z)$ defined below where the sample time is 0.2 seconds.

$$H(z) = \begin{bmatrix} \dfrac{1}{z+0.3} & \dfrac{z}{z+0.3} \\ \dfrac{-z+2}{z+0.3} & \dfrac{3}{z+0.3} \end{bmatrix}$$

```
>> nums = {1 [1 0];[-1 2] 3}
Ts = 0.2
H = tf(nums,[1 0.3],Ts)
```

nums =

```
    [      1.00]   [1x2 double]
    [1x2 double]   [      3.00]
```

Ts =

```
          0.20
```

Transfer function from input 1 to output...
```
          1
 #1:   -------
       z + 0.3


       -z + 2
 #2:   -------
       z + 0.3
```

Transfer function from input 2 to output...
```
          z
 #1:   -------
       z + 0.3


          3
 #2:   -------
       z + 0.3
```

Sampling time: 0.2

EXERCISE 3-3

Given the zero-pole-gain model

$$H(z) = \frac{z - 0.7}{z - 0.5}$$

with sample time 0.01 seconds, perform a resampling to 0.05 seconds. Then undo the resampling and verify that you obtain the original model.

```
>> H = zpk(0.7,0.5,1,0.1)
H2 = d2d(H,0.05)
```

Zero/pole/gain:

```
(z-0.7)
-------
(z-0.5)
```

Sampling time: 0.1

Zero/pole/gain:

```
(z-0.8243)
----------
(z-0.7071)
```

Sampling time: 0.05

We reverse the resampling in the following way:

```
>> d2d(H2,0.1)
```

Zero/pole/gain:

```
(z-0.7)
-------
(z-0.5)
```

Sampling time: 0.1

Thus the original model is obtained.

EXERCISE 3-4

Consider the continuous fourth-order model given by the transfer function *h*(*s*) defined below. Reduce the order by eliminating the states corresponding to small values of the diagonal balanced grammian vector g. Compare the original and reduced models.

$$h(s) = \frac{s^3 + 11s^2 + 36s + 26}{s^4 + 14.6s^3 + 74.96s^2 + 153.7s + 99.65}$$

We start by defining the model and computing a balanced state-space realization as follows:

```
>> h = tf([1 11 36 26],[1 14.6 74.96 153.7 99.65])
[hb,g] = balreal(h)
g'
```

Transfer function:

```
        s^3 + 11 s^2 + 36s + 26
--------------------------------------------
s^4 + 14.6 s^3 + 74.96 s^2 + 153.7s + 99.65
```

```
a =
            x1        x2        x3        x4
   x1    -3.601   -0.8212   -0.6163    0.05831
   x2     0.8212   -0.593    -1.027    0.09033
   x3    -0.6163    1.027    -5.914     1.127
   x4    -0.05831  0.09033   -1.127    -4.492
```

```
b =
             u1
   x1    -1.002
   x2     0.1064
   x3    -0.08612
   x4    -0.008112
```

```
c =
            x1        x2        x3        x4
   y1    -1.002   -0.1064   -0.08612   0.008112
```

```
d =
        u1
   y1   0
```

Continuous-time model.

```
g =

    0.1394
    0.0095
    0.0006
    0.0000
ans =

    0.1394    0.0095    0.0006    0.0000
```

We now remove the three states corresponding to the last three values of *g* using two different methods.

```
>> hmdc = modred(hb,2:4,'mdc')
hdel = modred(hb,2:4,'del')

a =
            x1
   x1   -4.655

b =
            u1
   x1   -1.139

c =
            x1
   y1   -1.139

d =
            u1
   y1   -0.01786

Continuous-time model.

a =
            x1
   x1   -3.601

b =
            u1
   x1   -1.002

c =
            x1
   y1   -1.002

d =
        u1
   y1   0

Continuous-time model.
```

Next we compare the responses with the original model (see Figure 3-27).

```
>> bode(h,'-',hmdc,'x',hdel,'*')
```

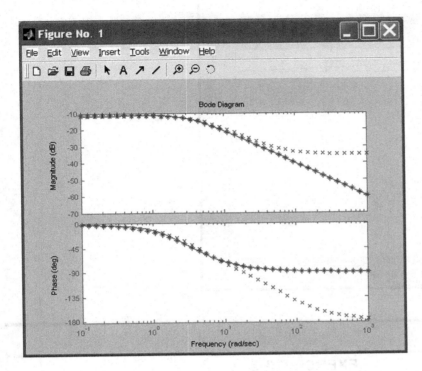

Figure 3-27.

We see that in both cases the reduced model is better than the original. We now compare the step responses (see Figure 3-28)

```
>> step(h,'-',hmdc,'-.',hdel,'--')
```

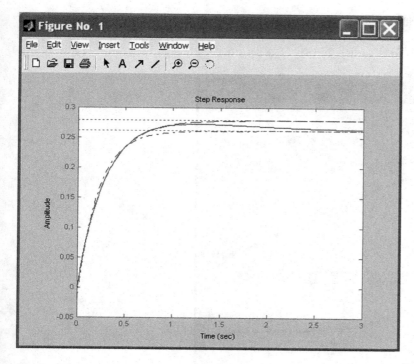

Figure 3-28.

EXERCISE 3-5

Calculate the covariance of response of the discrete SISO system defined by $H(z)$ and T_s below, corresponding to a Gaussian white noise of intensity $W = 5$.

$$H(z) = \frac{2z+1}{z^2 + 0.2z + 0.5}, \ T_s = 0.1$$

```
>> sys = tf([2 1],[1 0.2 0.5],0.1)
```

```
Transfer function:
    2 z + 1
-----------------
z^2 + 0.2 z + 0.5
```

```
Sampling time: 0.1
>>p = covar(sys,5)
```

```
p =
```

```
30.3167
```

EXERCISE 3-6

Plot the poles and zeros of the continuous-time transfer function system defined by

$$H(s) = \frac{2s^2 + 5s + 1}{s^2 + 2s + 3}.$$

```
>> H = tf([2 5 1],[1 2 3])
Transfer function:

2 s^2 + 5s + 1
--------------
s ^ 2 + 2s + 3

>> pzmap (H)
>> sgrid
```

Figure 3-29 shows the result.

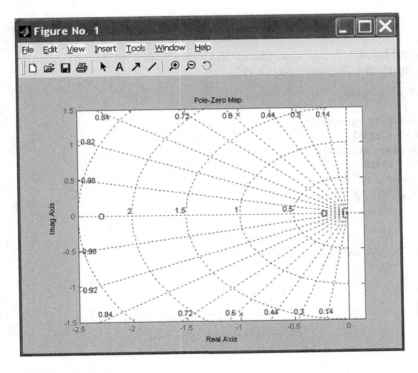

Figure 3-29.

EXERCISE 3-7

Consider the diagram in Figure 3-30 in which the matrices of the state-space model sys2 are given by:

$$A = [-9.0201, 17.7791; -1.6943, 3.2138];$$
$$B = [-.5112, .5362; -0.002, -1.8470];$$
$$C = [-3.2897, 2.4544; -13.5009, 18.0745];$$
$$D = [-.5476, -.1410; -.6459, .2958].$$

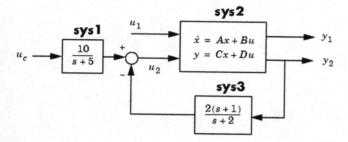

Figure 3-30.

First join the unconnected blocks, and secondly find the state-space model for the global interconnection given by the matrix Q = [3.1, − 4; 4,3,0] with inputs = [1,2] and outputs = [2,3].

The blocks are joined using the following syntax:

```
>> A = [ -9.0201,  17.7791; -1.6943  3.2138 ];
B = [ -.5112,  .5362;  -.002  -1.8470];
C = [ -3.2897,  2.4544;  -13.5009  18.0745];
D = [-.5476,  -.1410;  -.6459  .2958 ];
>> sys1 = tf(10,[1 5],'inputname','uc')
sys2 = ss(A,B,C,D,'inputname',{'u1' 'u2'},...
'outputname',{'y1' 'y2'})
sys3 = zpk(-1,-2,2)
```

Transfer function from input "uc" to output:

```
  10
 -----
 s + 5

a =

          x1      x2
    x1   -9.02    17.78
    x2   -1.694   3.214

b =

           u1       u2
    x1   -0.5112   0.5362
    x2   -0.002    -1.847
```

```
c =
          x1     x2
    y1   -3.29  2.454
    y2   -13.5  18.07

d =
           u1      u2
    y1   -0.5476  -0.141
    y2   -0.6459   0.2958
```

Continuous-time model.

Zero/pole/gain:

```
2 (s+1)
-------
(s+2)
```

The union of the unconnected blocks is created as follows:

sys = append(sys1,sys2,sys3)
```
a =
          x1      x2      x3      x4
    x1    -5       0       0       0
    x2     0    -9.02   17.78      0
    x3     0   -1.694   3.214      0
    x4     0       0       0      -2

b =
          uc      u1      u2       ?
    x1     4       0       0       0
    x2     0   -0.5112  0.5362     0
    x3     0   -0.002   -1.847     0
    x4     0       0       0     1.414

c =
          x1      x2      x3      x4
    ?     2.5      0       0       0
    y1     0    -3.29   2.454      0
    y2     0    -13.5   18.07      0
    ?      0       0       0    -1.414

d =
          uc      u1      u2       ?
    ?      0       0       0       0
    y1     0   -0.5476  -0.141     0
    y2     0   -0.6459   0.2958    0
    ?      0       0       0       2
```

Continuous-time model.

We then obtain the state-space model for the global interconnection.

```
>> Q = [3, 1, -4; 4, 3, 0];
>> inputs = [1 2];
>> outputs = [2 3];
>> sysc = connect(sys,Q,inputs,outputs)
```

```
a =
            x1        x2        x3        x4
    x1      -5         0         0         0
    x2    0.8422    0.07664    5.601    0.4764
    x3    -2.901    -33.03     45.16    -1.641
    x4    0.6571     -12       16.06    -1.628

b =
             uc        u1
    x1       4          0
    x2       0       -0.076
    x3       0       -1.501
    x4       0       -0.5739

c =
            x1        x2        x3        x4
    y1    -0.2215    -5.682    5.657    -0.1253
    y2    0.4646     -8.483    11.36    0.2628

d =
             uc        u1
    y1       0       -0.662
    y2       0       -0.4058
```

Continuous-time model.

EXERCISE 3-8

Plot the unit impulse response of the second-order state-space model defined below and store the results in an array with output response and simulation time.

The model is defined as follows:

$$\begin{bmatrix} \dot{x}_1 \\ \dot{x}_2 \end{bmatrix} = \begin{bmatrix} -0.5572 & -0.7814 \\ 0.7814 & 0 \end{bmatrix} \begin{bmatrix} x_1 \\ x_2 \end{bmatrix} + \begin{bmatrix} 1 & -1 \\ 0 & 2 \end{bmatrix} \begin{bmatrix} u_1 \\ u_2 \end{bmatrix}$$

The requested plot is obtained by using the following syntax (see Figure 3-31):

```
>> a = [-0.5572 -0.7814;0.7814  0];
b = [1 -1;0 2];
c = [1.9691  6.4493];
sys = ss(a,b,c,0);
impulse (sys)
```

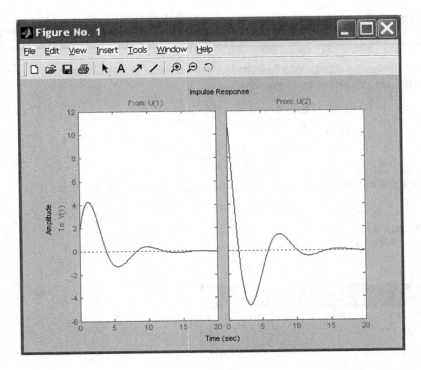

Figure 3-31.

The output response and simulation time are obtained using the syntax:

>> [y t] = impulse (sys)

$y(:,:,1)$ =

1.9691
2.6831
3.2617
3.7059
4.0197
4.2096
.
.

$y(:,:,2)$ =

10.9295
9.4915
7.9888
6.4622
4.9487
.
.

EXERCISE 3-9

Graph and simulate the response of the system with transfer function $H(s)$ defined below to a square signal of period 4 seconds, sampling every 0.1 seconds and every 10 seconds.

$$H(s) = \begin{bmatrix} \dfrac{2s^2 + 5s + 1}{s^2 + 2s + 3} \\ \dfrac{s-1}{s^2 + s + 5} \end{bmatrix}$$

We begin by generating the square signal with *gensys* and then perform the simulation using *lsim* (see Figure 3-32) as follows:

```
>> [u,t] = gensig('square',4,10,0.1);
>> H = [tf([2 5 1],[1 2 3]) ; tf([1 -1],[1 1 5])]
lsim(H,u,t)
```

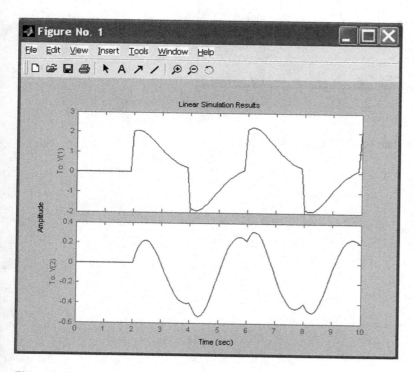

Figure 3-32.

Transfer function from input to output...

```
     2 s ^ 2 + 5 s + 1
#1:  ---------------
     s ^ 2 + 2 s + 3


          s 1
#2:  -----------
     s ^ 2 + s + 5
```

CHAPTER 4

■ ■ ■

Robust Predictive Control

Predictive Control Strategies: The Model Predictive Control Toolbox

The *Model Predictive Control Toolbox* is a complete set of tools which can be used to implement model predictive control strategies. Model predictive control strategies are often used in chemical engineering and in other industries.

The most important characteristics of this toolbox are:

- Modeling, identification and validation.
- Support for MISO, MIMO, step response and state-space models.
- Analysis of systems.
- Conversion between state-space, transfer function and step response models.

Model predictive control approximates a linear dynamic plant model to predict future changes and the effect of manipulating variables. The *online* optimization problem is formulated as a quadratic program which is resolved repeatedly using the most recent measurements.

The *Model Predictive Control Toolbox* includes more than 50 specialized MATLAB functions which help you to design, analze and simulate dynamical systems using a model predictive control approach. The toolbox supports finite step (or impulse) response, discrete and continuous-time transfer function and state-space formats. The toolbox handles non-square systems and supports a wide variety of state estimation techniques. Simulation tools test systems response with or without restrictions. For the identification of models, the toolbox has an interface that makes it easy to use models developed using the system identification toolbox.

ID Commands

[mx, ax, stdx] = autosc (x) **sx = scal(x,mx)** **sx = scal(x,mx,stdx)** **rx = rescal(x,mx)** **rx = rescal(x,mx,stdx)**	*Scales an input matrix or vector x by its column means (mx) and standard deviations (stdx) automatically and outputs mx and stdx as options. By using scal, the input can also be scaled by some specified means and/or standard deviations. rescal converts scaled data back to the original data.*
plant = imp2step(delt,nout,theta1, theta2,..., theta25)	*Builds a MIMO (multi-input multi-output) model in MPC step format. Each thetai is an n×m matrix corresponding to the impulse response coefficients for output i. n is the number of the coefficients and m is the number of inputs. delt is the sampling interval used for obtaining the impulse response coefficients. nout is the output stability indicator.*

(continued)

[theta, yres] = mlr (xreg, yreg, ninput) **[theta, yres] = mlr (xreg yreg, ninput, plotopt, wtheta, wdeltheta)**	*Determines impulse response coefficients for a multi-input single-output system via Multivariable Least Squares Regression or Ridge Regression. xreg and yreg are the input matrix and output vector produced by routines such as wrtreg. ninput is number of inputs. Least Squares is used to determine the impulse response coefficient matrix, theta. Columns of theta correspond to impulse response coefficients from each input. Optional output yres is the vector of residuals, the difference between the actual outputs and the predicted outputs.* *Optional inputs include plotopt, wtheta, and wdeltheta. No plot is produced if plotopt is equal to 0 which is the default; a plot of the actual output and the predicted output is produced ifplotopt=1; two plots -- plot of actual and predicted output, and plot of residuals -- are produced for plotopt=2. Penalties on the squares of theta and the changes in theta can be specified through the scalar weights wtheta and wdeltheta, respectively (defaults are 0).*
[theta, yres, w, cw, ssqdif] = plsr(xreg,yreg,ninput,lv) **[theta, yres, w, cw, ssqdif] = plsr(xreg,yreg,ninput,lv, plotopt)**	*Determines the impulse response coefficients for a multi-input single-output system via Partial Least Squares (PLS).*
yres = validmod (xreg, yreg, theta) **yres = validmod (xreg yreg, theta, plotopt)**	*Validates an impulse response model for a new set of data.*
[xreg, yreg] = wrtreg (x, y, n)	*Writes input and output data matrices for a multi-input single-output system so that they can be used in regression routines mlr and pls for determining impulse response coefficients.*

Information Matrix Plotting Commands

mpcinfo(mat)	*Returns information about the type and size of the matrix mat.*
plotall(y,u) **plotall(y,u,t)**	*Plots outputs and manipulated variables from a simulation. Input variables y and u are matrices of outputs and manipulated variables, respectively. (t = period).*
plotfrsp(vmat) **plotfrsp(vmat,out,in)**	*Plots the frequency response generated by mod2frsp as a Bode plot. vmat is the array containing the data.*
ploteach(y) **ploteach(y, u)** **ploteach([ ], u)** **ploteach(y, [], t)** **ploteach([], u, t)** **ploteach(y, u, t)**	*Plots outputs and manipulated variables from a simulation on separate graphs. Input variables y and u are matrices of outputs and manipulated variables, respectively. (t = period).*
plotstep(plant) **plotstep(plant,opt)**	*Plots multiple step responses. plant is a step-response matrix in the MPC step format created by mod2step, ss2step or tfd2step. opt is an optional scalar or row vector that allows you to select the outputs to be plotted.*

Model Conversion Commands

c2dmp	*Converts a state-space model from continuous-time to discrete-time. (Equivalent to c2d in the Control System Toolbox)*
[numd,dend] = cp2dp(num,den,delt) **[numd,dend] = cp2dp(num,den,delt,delay)**	*Converts a single-input-single-output, continuous-time transfer function in standard MATLAB polynomial form (including an optional time delay) to a sampled-data transfer function. (delt is the sampling period and delay is the time delay.)*
d2cmp	*Convertsa state-space model from discrete-time to continuous-time. (Equivalent to d2c in the Control System Toolbox.)*
newmod = mod2mod (oldmod, delt2)	*Changes the sampling period of a model in MPC mod format. oldmod is the existing model in MPC mod format. delt2 is the new sampling period for the model.*
[phi,gam,c,d] = mod2ss(mod) **[phi,gam,c,d,minfo] = mod2ss(mod)**	*Extracts the standard discrete-time state-space matrices and other information from a model stored in the MPC mod format.*
plant = mod2step(mod,tfinal) **[plant,dplant] = mod2step(mod,tfinal,delt2,nout)**	*Uses a model in the mod format to calculate the step response of a SISO or MIMO system in MPC step format.*
g = poly2tfd(num,den) **g = poly2tfd(num,den,delt,delay)**	*Converts a transfer function (continuous or discrete) from the standard MATLAB poly format into the MPC tf format.*
pmod = ss2mod(phi,gam,c,d) **pmod = ss2mod(phi,gam,c,d,minfo)**	*Converts a discrete-time state-space system model into the MPC mod format.*
plant = ss2step(phi,gam,c,d,tfinal) **plant = ss2step(phi,gam,c,d,tfinal,delt1,delt2,nout)**	*Uses a model in state-space format to calculate the step response of a SISO or MIMO system, in MPC step format.*
ss2tf2	*Converts state-space model to transfer function. (Equivalent to ss2tf in the Control System Toolbox.)*
tf2ssm	*Converts a transfer function to a state-space model. (Equivalent to t f2ss in the Control System Toolbox.)*
model = tfd2mod(delt2,ny,g1,g2,g3,...,g25)	*Converts a transfer function (continuous or discrete) from the MPC tf format into the MPC mod format, converting to discrete time if necessary.*
plant = tfd2step(tfinal,delt2,nout,g1) **plant = tfd2step(tfinal,delt2,nout,g1,...,g25)**	*Calculates the MIMO step response of a model in the MPC tf format. The resulting step response is in the MPC step format.*
umod = th2mod(th) **[umod,emod] = th2mod(th1,th2,...,thN)**	*Converts a SISO or MISO model from the theta format (as used in the System Identification Toolbox) to one in the MPC mod format. Can also combine such models to form a MIMO system.*

Model Building Commands - MPC Mod Format

model = addmd (pmod, dmod)	*Adds one or more measured disturbances to a plant model in the MPC mod format.*
pmod = addmod (mod1, mod2)	*Combines two models in the MPC mod format such that the output of one combines with the manipulated inputs of the other.*
model = addumd (pmod, dmod)	*Adds one or more unmeasured disturbances to a plant model in MPC mod format.*
pmod = appmod (mod1, mod2)	*Appends two models to form a composite model that retains the inputs and outputs of the original models.*
pmod = paramod (mod1, mod2)	*Puts two models in parallel by connecting their outputs.*
pmod = sermod (mod1, mod2)	*Puts two models in series by connecting the output of one to the input of the other.*

Control Design and Simulation Commands - MPC Step Format

yp = cmpc(plant,model,ywt,uwt,M,P,tend,r) **[yp,u,ym] = cmpc(plant,model,ywt,uwt,M,P,tend,...)**	*Simulates closed-loop systems with hard bounds on manipulated variables and/or outputs using models in the MPC step format. Solves the MPC optimization problem by quadratic programming.*
[clmod] = mpccl(plant,model,Kmpc) **[clmod,cmod] = mpccl(plant,model,Kmpc,tfilter,...** **dplant, dmodel)**	*Combines a plant model and a controller model in MPC step format, yielding a closed-loop system model in the MPC mod format.*
KMPC = mpccon (model) **KMPC = mpccon (model, ywt uwt, M, P)**	*Calculates MPC controller gain using a model in MPC step format.*
yp = mpcsim(plant,model,Kmpc,tend,r) **[yp,u,ym] = mpcsim(plant,model,Kmpc,tend,r,usat,...** **tfilter, dplant, dmodel, dstep)**	*Simulates closed-loop systems with saturation constraints on the manipulated variables using models in the MPC step format.*
nlcmpc	*Model predictive controller for simulating closed-loop systems with hard bounds on manipulated variables and/or controlled variables using linear models in the MPC step format for nonlinear plants represented as Simulink S-functions.*
nlmpcsim	*Model predictive controller for simulating closed-loop systems with saturation constraints on the manipulated variables using linear models in the MPC step format for nonlinear plants represented as Simulink S-functions.*

Control Design and Simulation Commands - MPC Mod Format

yp = scmpc(pmod,imod,ywt,uwt,M,P,tend,r) [yp,u,ym] = scmpc(pmod,imod,ywt,uwt,M,P,tend, ... r,ulim,ylim,Kest,z,d,w,wu)	*Simulates closed-loop systems with hard bounds on manipulated variables and/or outputs using models in the MPC mod format. Solves the MPC optimization problem by quadratic programming.*
[clmod,cmod] = smpccl(pmod,imod,Ks) [clmod,cmod] = smpccl(pmod,imod,Ks,Kest)	*Combines a plant model and a controller model in the MPC mod format, yielding a closed-loop system model in the MPC format.*
Ks = smpccon(imod) Ks = smpccon(imod,ywt,uwt,M,P)	*Calculates MPC controller gain using a model in MPC mod format.*
[Kest] = smpcest(imod,Q,R)	*Sets up a state-estimator gain matrix for use with MPC controller design and simulation routines using models in the MPC mod format.*
yp = smpcsim(pmod,imod,Ks,tend,r) [yp,u,ym] = smpcsim(pmod,imod,Ks,tend,r,usat,... Kest, z, d, w, wu)	*Simulates closed-loop systems with saturation constraints on the manipulated variables using models in the MPC mod format.*

Script Analysis Commands

frsp = mod2frsp(mod,freq) [frsp,eyefrsp] = mod2frsp(mod,freq,out,in,balflg)	*Calculates the complex frequency response of a system in MPC mod format.*
g = smpcgain(mod) poles = smpcpole(mod)	*Calculates the steady-state gain matrix or poles for a system in the MPC mod format.*
[sigma, omega] = svdfrsp (vmat)	*Calculates the singular values of a varying matrix, for example, the frequency response generated by mod2frsp.*

Robust Control Systems: The Robust Control Toolbox

The *Robust Control Toolbox* provides tools for the design and analysis of robust multivariate control systems. It includes systems in which it is possible to model errors, and dynamic systems with uncertain elements or with parameters that can vary during the life of the product. The powerful algorithms included in this toolbox allow you to run complex calculations, allowing for a large number of variations in the parameters.

The most important characteristics of this toolbox are:

- H^2 and H_∞ control based on LQG (synthesis).

- Multivariate frequency response.

- Construction of state-space models.

- Unique values based on model conversion.

- Reduction of high-order models.

- Spectral and inner-outer factorization.

Optional Data Structure System Commands

[b1,b2,...,bn] = branch(tr,PATH1, PATH2,...,PATHN)	*Recovers the matrices packed in a mksys or tree variable selectively. The branches returned are determined by the paths PATH1, PATH2,..., PATHN.*
TR = graft(TR1,B) **TR = graft(TR1,B,NM)**	*Adds root branch B onto a tree variable TR1 (previously created by tree or mksys). If TR1 has N branches, then the numerical index of the new branch is N+1; and the numerical indices of other root branches are unchanged.*
[i,TY,N] = issystem(S)	*Returns a value for i of either 1 (true) or 0 (false) depending on whether or not the variable S is a system created by the function mksys. Also returned is the type of system TY and the number N of variable names associated with a system of type TY, except that if S is not a system then TY = [ ]; and N = 0.*
[i] = istree(T) **[i,b] = istree(T,path)**	*Checks whether a variable T is a tree or not. When the second input argument path is present, the function istree checks the existence of the branch specified by path.*
S = mksys(a,b,c,d) **S = mksys(v1,v2,v3,vn, TY)**	*Packs several matrices describing a system of type TY into a MATLAB variable S, under "standard" variable names determined by the value of the string TY.*
T = tree(nm,b1,b2,bn)	*Creates a tree data structure T containing several variables and their names.*
[VARS,N] = vrsys(NAM)	*Returns a string VARS and an integer N where VARS contains the list (separated by commas) of the N names of the matrices associated with a system described by the string name NAM.*

Modeling Commands

[a,b1,b2,c1,c2,d11,d12,d21,d22] = ... **augss(ag,bg,aw1,bw1,aw2,bw2,aw3,bw3)** **[a,b1,b2,c1,c2,d11,d12,d21,d22] = ...** **augss(ag,bg,aw1,bw1,aw2,bw2,aw3,bw3,w3poly)** **[a,b1,b2,c1,c2,d11,d12,d21,d22] = ...** **augtf(ag,bg,cg,dg,w1,w2,w3)** **[tss] = augss(ssg,ssw1,ssw2,ssw3,w3poly)** **[tss] = augtf(ssg,w1,w2,w3)** **[tss] = augss(ssg,ssw1,ssw2,ssw3)**	*State-space or transfer function plant augmentation for use in weighted mixed-sensitivity H2 and H∞ design.*
[acl,bcl,ccl,dcl] = interc(a,b,c,d,m,n,f) **[sscl] = interc(ss,m,n,f)**	*Multivariate general interconnection of systems.*

Model Conversion Commands

[ab,bb,cb,db] = bilin(a,b,c,d,ver,type,aug) **[ssb] = bilin(ss,ver,type,aug)**	*Computes the effect on a system of the frequency-variable substitution* $$s = \frac{\alpha z + \delta}{\gamma z + \beta}.$$ *The variable ver is either 1 (forward transform: s to z) or -1 (reverse transform: z to s) (S or z). The variable type denotes the type of bilinear transformation and can be 'BwdRec' (backward rectangular), 'FwdRec' (forward rectangular), 'S_Tust' (shifted Tustin), 'S_ftjw' (shifted jw-axis, bilinear pole-shifting, continuous-time to continuous-time) or 'G_Bilin' (general bilinear, continuous-time to continuous-time). aug = [$\alpha, \beta, \gamma, \delta$].*
[aa, bb, cc, dd] = des2ss(a,b,c,d,E,k) **[ss1] = des2ss (ss, E, k)**	*Converts a descriptor system into SVD state-space form.*
[a,b1,b2,c1,c2,d11,d12,d21,d22] = **lftf(A,B1,B2,a,b1,b2,)** **[aa,bb,cc,dd] =** **lftf(a,b1,b2,c1,c2,d11,d12,d21,d22,aw,bw,cw,dw)** **[aa,bb,cc,dd] =** **lftf(aw,bw,cw,dw,a,b1,b2,c1,c2,d11,d12,d21,d22)** **tss = lftf(tss1,tss2)** **ss = lftf(tss1,ss2)** **ss = lftf(ss1,tss2)**	*Two-port or one-port state-space linear fractional transformation.*
[ag,bg1,dg22,at,bt1,dt21,dt22] = **sectf(af,bf1,df22,secf,secg)** **[ag,bg,cg,dg,at,bt1,dt21,dt22] =** **sectf(af,bf,cf,df,secf,secg)** **[tssg,tsst] = sectf(tssf,secf,secg)** **[ssg,tsst] = sectf(ssf,secf,secg)**	*State-space sector bilinear transformation.*
[a1,b1,c1,d1,a2,b2,c2,d2,m] = stabproj(a,b,c,d) **[a1,b1,c1,d1,a2,b2,c2,d2] = slowfast(a,b,c,d,cut)** **[ss1,ss2,m] = stabproj(ss)** **[ss1,ss2] = slowfast(ss,cut)**	*Stable and antistable projection. Slow and fast modes decomposition.*
[a,b,c,d] = tfm2ss(num,den,r,c) **[ss] = tfm2ss(tf,r,c)**	*Converts a transfer function matrix (MIMO) into state-space form.*

Utility Commands

[p1,p2,lamp,perr,wellposed,p] = aresolv(a,q,r)	*Solves the continuous generalized Riccati equation* $A^TP + PA - PRP + Q = 0$ *where* $P = p = p^1/p^2$.
[p1,p2,lamp,perr,wellposed,p] = aresolv(a,q,r,Type)	*Solves the discrete generalized Riccati equation*
[p1,p2,lamp,perr,wellposed,p] = daresolv(a,b,q,r)	$A^TPA - P - A^TPB(R + B^TPB)^{-1}B^TPA + Q = 0$ *where* $P = p + p^2/p^1$ *is the solution for which the eigenvalues of* $A - RP$ *are*
[p1,p2,lamp,perr,wellposed,p] = daresolv(a,b,q,r,Type)	*inside the unit disk.*
[tot] = riccond(a,b,qrn,p1,p2)	*Provides the condition numbers of the continuous Riccati equation.*
[tot] = driccond(a,b,q,r,p1,p2)	*Provides the condition numbers of the discrete Riccati equation.*
[v,t,m] = blkrsch(a,Type,cut)	*Block ordered real Schur form.*
[v,t,m,swap] = cschur(a,Type)	*Ordered complex Schur form via complex Givens rotation.*

Commands for Bode Multivariate Graphics

[cg, ph, w] = cgloci (a, b, c, d(,Ts)) [cg, ph, w] = cgloci (a, b, c, d(,Ts), 'inv') [cg, ph, w] = cgloci (a, b, c, d(,Ts), w) [cg, ph, w] = cgloci (a, b, c, d(,Ts), w, 'inv')[cg, ph, w] = cgloci (ss)	*Continuous characteristic gain loci frequency response.*
[cg, ph, w] = dcgloci (a, b, c, d(,Ts)) [cg, ph, w] = dcgloci (a, b, c, d(,Ts), 'inv') [cg, ph, w] = dcgloci (a, b, c, d(,Ts), w) [cg, ph, w] = dcgloci (a, b, c, d(,Ts), w, 'inv') [cg, ph, w] = dcgloci (ss)	*Discrete characteristic gain loci frequency response.*
[sv,w] = dsigma(a,b,c,d(,Ts)) [sv,w] = dsigma(a,b,c,d(,Ts),'inv') [sv,w] = dsigma(a,b,c,d(,Ts),w) [sv,w] = dsigma(a,b,c,d(,Ts),w,'inv') [sv, w] = dsigma (ss...)	*Computes the discrete version of the singular value Bode plot.*
[sv,w] = sigma(a,b,c,d(,Ts)) [sv,w] = sigma(a,b,c,d(,Ts),'inv') [sv,w] = sigma(a,b,c,d(,Ts),w) [sv,w] = sigma(a,b,c,d(,Ts),w,'inv') [sv, w] = sigma (ss...)	*Computes the singular value Bode plot.*
[mu,ascaled,logm,x] = muopt(a) [mu,ascaled,logm,x] = muopt(a,k)	*Computes an upper bound on the structured singular value using the multiplier approach.*
[mu,ascaled,logd] = osborne(a) [mu,ascaled,logd] = osborne(a,k)	*Computes an upper bound on the structured singular value via the Osborne method.*
[mu] = perron (a) [mu] = perron (a, k) [mu,ascaled,logd] = psv(a) [mu,ascaled,logd] = psv(a,k)	*Computes an upper bound on the structured singular value via the Perron eigenvector method.*
[mu,logd] = ssv(a,b,c,d,w) [mu,logd] = ssv(a,b,c,d,w,k) [mu,logd] = ssv(a,b,c,d,w,k,opt) [mu,logd] = ssv(ss,)	*Computes the structured singular value (multivariable stability margin) Bode plot.*

EXERCISE 4-1

Given the double-input single-output model *y(s)* defined below, whose input and output data are in the mlrdat file, determine the standard deviation of the input data using the autoesc function and scale the input by its standard deviation only. Arrange the input and output data in a form which allows you to calculate the impulse response coefficients (35 coefficients) and find these coefficients using mlr. Finally, scale theta based on the standard deviation of the input, convert the model to MPC step format and plot the step response coefficients.

$$y(s) = \begin{bmatrix} \dfrac{5.72e^{-14s}}{60s+1} & \dfrac{1.52e^{-15s}}{25s+1} \end{bmatrix} \begin{bmatrix} u_1(s) \\ u_2(s) \end{bmatrix}$$

The following MATLAB syntax is used to generate the plots shown in Figure 4-1:

```
>> load mlrdat;
>> [ax, mx, stdx] = autosc (x);
>> mx = [0,0];
sx = scal(x,mx,stdx);
>> n = 35;
[xreg, yreg] = wrtreg (sx, y, n);
>> ninput = 2;
plotopt = 2;
[theta, yres] = mlr (xreg, yreg, ninput, plotopt);
```

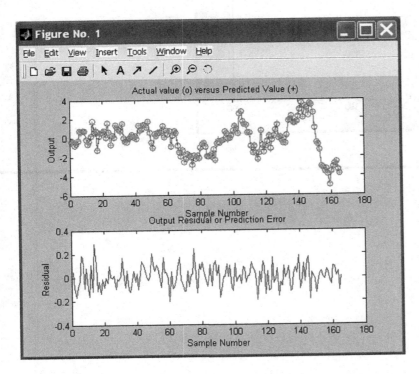

Figure 4-1.

The scaling of theta, model conversion and plotting of the step response coefficients (see Figure 4-2), with a sample time of 7 minutes to find the impulse, uses the following syntax:

```
>> theta = scal(theta,mx,stdx);
>> nout = 1;
delt = 7;
model = imp2step(delt,nout,theta);
>> plotstep (model)
```

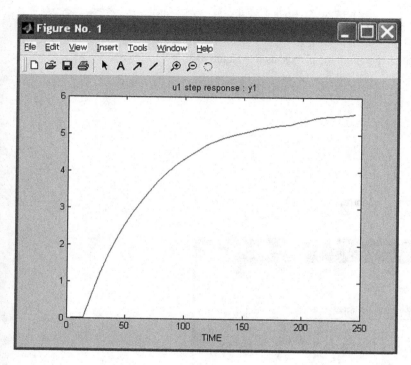

Figure 4-2.

EXERCISE 4-2

Convert the continuous-time transfer function model *G(s)* defined below to the corresponding MPC transfer function model. Perform the same task, assuming a delay of 2.5, and find the equivalent discrete transfer function.

The model *G(s)* without delay is defined as:

$$\frac{3s-1}{5s^2+2s+1}$$

which is converted into transfer function format as follows:

```
>> g = poly2tfd(0.5*[3 -1],[5 2 1])

g =
          0     1.5000    -0.5000
     5.0000     2.0000     1.0000
          0          0          0
```

If there is a delay of 2.5 the model is represented as:

$$\frac{3s-1}{5s^2+2s+1}e^{-2.5s}$$

and the conversion to transfer function format is as follows:

```
>> g = poly2tfd(0.5*[3 -1],[5 2 1],0,2.5)

g =

          0     1.5000    -0.5000
     5.0000     2.0000     1.0000
          0     2.5000          0
```

To find the equivalent discrete transform function using a sampling period of 0.75 units, use the following syntax:

```
>> delt=0.75;
[numd,dend]=cp2dp(0.5*[3 -1],[5 2 1],delt,rem(2.5,delt))

numd =

0.1232 0 - 0.1106 - 0.0607

DEnd =

1.0000 - 1.6445 0.7408 0
```

EXERCISE 4-3

Given the following system build separate variables to create response models u and w with a sample time of $T=3$ and combine them to form a model of the complete system.

$$\begin{bmatrix} y_1(s) \\ y_2(s) \end{bmatrix} = \begin{bmatrix} \dfrac{12.8e^{s}}{16.7s+1} & \dfrac{-18.9e^{-3s}}{21.0s+1} \\[2ex] \dfrac{6.6^{e-7s}}{10.9s+1} & \dfrac{-19.4^{e-3s}}{14.4s+1} \end{bmatrix} \begin{bmatrix} u_1(s) \\ u_2(s) \end{bmatrix} + \begin{bmatrix} \dfrac{3.8e^{-8s}}{14.9s+1} \\[2ex] \dfrac{4.9e^{-3s}}{13.2s+1} \end{bmatrix} w(s)$$

```
>> g11=poly2tfd(12.8,[16.7 1],0,1);
g21=poly2tfd(6.6,[10.9 1],0,7);
g12=poly2tfd(-18.9,[21.0 1],0,3);
g22=poly2tfd(-19.4,[14.4 1],0,3);
delt=3; ny=2;
umod=tfd2mod(delt,ny,g11,g21,g12,g22);
gw1=poly2tfd(3.8,[14.9 1],0,8);
gw2=poly2tfd(4.9,[13.2 1],0,3);
wmod=tfd2mod(delt,ny,gw1,gw2);
pmod=addumd(umod,wmod)

pmod =

Columns 1 through 14
```

```
3.0000  13.0000   2.0000        0   1.0000   2.0000        0        0        0        0        0        0        0        0
   NaN   1.5950  -0.6345        0        0        0        0        0        0        0        0        0        0        0
     0   1.0000        0        0        0        0        0        0        0        0        0        0        0        0
     0        0   1.0000        0        0        0        0        0        0        0        0        0        0        0
     0        0        0   1.0000        0        0        0        0        0        0        0        0        0        0
     0        0        0        0   1.0000        0        0        0        0        0        0        0        0        0
     0        0        0        0        0        0   1.6788  -0.7038        0        0        0        0        0        0
     0        0        0        0        0        0   1.0000        0        0        0        0        0        0        0
     0        0        0        0        0        0        0   1.0000        0        0        0        0        0        0
     0        0        0        0        0        0        0        0   1.6143  -0.6514        0        0        0        0
     0        0        0        0        0        0        0        0   1.0000        0        0        0        0        0
     0        0        0        0        0        0        0        0        0   1.0000        0        0        0        0
     0        0        0        0        0        0        0        0        0        0   1.0000        0        0        0
     0        0        0        0        0        0        0        0        0        0        0   1.0000        0        0
     0   1.4447  -0.4371  -0.5012        0        0        0  -2.5160   2.0428        0        0   0.2467   0.2498  -0.3556
     0        0        0   1.1064  -0.4429  -0.4024        0  -3.6484   3.1627        0   0.9962  -0.8145        0        0
```

Columns 15 through 17

0	0	0
1.0000	0	0
0	0	0
0	0	0
0	0	0
0	0	0
0	1.0000	0
0	0	0
0	0	0
0	0	1.0000
0	0	0
0	0	0
0	0	0
0	0	0
0	0	0
0	0	0

EXERCISE 4-4

For the following system build individual variables to form the transfer function model and calculate and plot its MIMO step response.

$$\begin{bmatrix} y_1(s) \\ y_2(s) \end{bmatrix} = \begin{bmatrix} \dfrac{12.8e^s}{16.7s+1} & \dfrac{-18.9e^{-3s}}{21.0s+1} \\ \dfrac{6.6e^{-7s}}{10.9s+1} & \dfrac{-19.4e^{-3s}}{14.4s+1} \end{bmatrix} \begin{bmatrix} u_1(s) \\ u_2(s) \end{bmatrix} + \begin{bmatrix} \dfrac{3.8e^{-8s}}{14.9s+1} \\ \dfrac{4.9e^{-3s}}{13.2s+1} \end{bmatrix} w(s)$$

The following syntax is used to create the graph shown in Figure 4-3:

```
>> g11=poly2tfd(12.8,[16.7 1],0,1);
g21=poly2tfd(6.6,[10.9 1],0,7);
g12=poly2tfd(-18.9,[21.0 1],0,3);
g22=poly2tfd(-19.4,[14.4 1],0,3);
delt=3; ny=2; tfinal=90;
plant=tfd2step(tfinal,delt,ny,g11,g21,g12,g22,gw1,gw2);
plotstep(plant)
Percent error in the last step response coefficient
of output yi for input uj is :
0.48% 1.6% 0.41%
0.049% 0.24% 0.14%
```

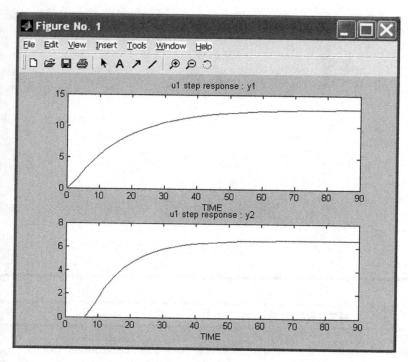

Figure 4-3.

For the linear system described in the previous problem, measure the effect of setting a limit of 0.1 in the exchange rate and a minimum of − 0.15 for u2 and u1. Then apply a lower limit of zero for both outputs.

We build the model using the following syntax:

```
>> g11=poly2tfd(12.8,[16.7 1],0,1);
g21=poly2tfd(6.6,[10.9 1],0,7);
g12=poly2tfd(-18.9,[21.0 1],0,3);
g22=poly2tfd(-19.4,[14.4 1],0,3);
delt=3; ny=2; tfinal=90;
model=tfd2step(tfinal,delt,ny,g11,g21,g12,g22);
plant=model;
P=6; M=2; ywt=[ ]; uwt=[1 1];
tend=30; r=[0 1];
Percent error in the last step response coefficient
of output yi for input uj is :
0.48% 1.6%
0.049% 0.24%
```

The effect of the restrictions can be seen using the following syntax (see Figure 4-4):

```
>> ulim=[-inf -0.15 inf inf 0.1 100];
ylim=[ ];
[y,u]=cmpc(plant,model,ywt,uwt,M,P,tend,r,ulim,ylim);
plotall(y,u,delt),pause
```

Time remaining 30/30
Time remaining 0/30
Simulation time is 0.03 seconds.

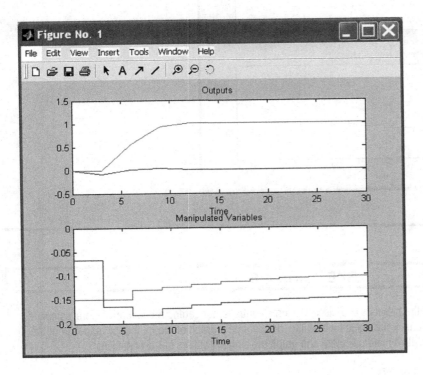

Figure 4-4.

A lower limit of zero is applied to both outputs by using the following syntax (see Figure 4-5):

```
>> ulim=[-inf -0.15 inf inf 0.1 100];
ylim=[0 0 inf inf];
[y,u]=cmpc(plant,model,ywt,uwt,M,P,tend,r,ulim,ylim);
plotall(y,u,delt),pause
```

Time remaining 30/30
Time remaining 0/30
Simulation time is 0.03 seconds.

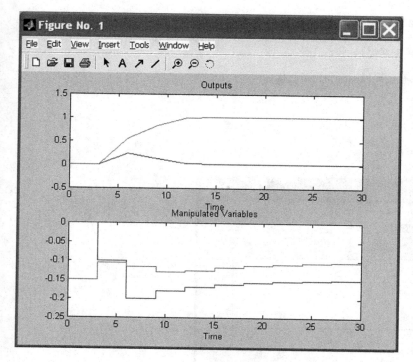

Figure 4-5.

EXERCISE 4-6

For the linear system described in the previous exercises, design a controller for setting model parameters, calculate the closed loop of the system and check the poles for stability. Then create a graph of the frequency response of the sensitivity and complementary sensitivity and calculate and graph the singular values of the sensitivity.

```
>> g11=poly2tfd(12.8,[16.7 1],0,1);
g21=poly2tfd(6.6,[10.9 1],0,7);
g12=poly2tfd(-18.9,[21.0 1],0,3);
g22=poly2tfd(-19.4,[14.4 1],0,3);
delt=3; ny=2;
imod=tfd2mod(delt,ny,g11,g21,g12,g22);
pmod=imod;

>> P=6;.
M=2;
ywt=[ ];
uwt=[ ];
Ks=smpccon(imod,ywt,uwt,M,P);
>> clmod=smpccl(pmod,imod,Ks);
maxpole=max(abs(smpcpole(clmod)))
```

maxpole =

0.8869

The graphs of the frequency response of the sensitivity (Figure 4-6) and complementary sensitivity (Figure 4-7) are generated as follows:

```
>> freq = [-3,0,30];
in = [1:ny]; % input is r for comp. sensitivity
out = [1:ny]; % output is yp for comp. sensitivity
[frsp,eyefrsp] = mod2frsp(clmod,freq,out,in);
plotfrsp(eyefrsp); % Sensitivity
pause;
```

over estimated time to perform the frequency response: 0.61 sec

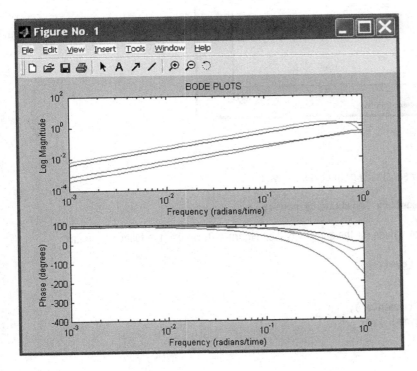

Figure 4-6.

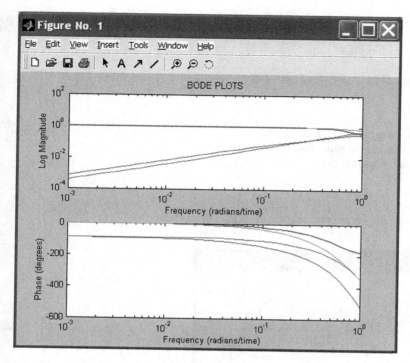

Figure 4-7.

The syntax for the complementary sensitivity graph is as follows:

```
>> plotfrsp(frsp); % Complementary Sensitivity pause;
```

To calculate and graph the singular values for the sensitivity (see Figure 4-8) we use the following syntax:

```
>> [sigma, omega] = svdfrsp (eyefrsp);
CLG;
semilogx(omega,sigma);
title('Singular Values vs. Frequency');
xlabel('Frequency (radians/time)');
ylabel('Singular Values');
```

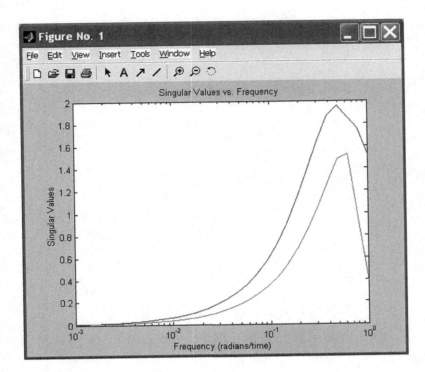

Figure 4-8.

Get the eBook for only $10!

Now you can take the weightless companion with you anywhere, anytime. Your purchase of this book entitles you to 3 electronic versions for only $10.

This Apress title will prove so indispensible that you'll want to carry it with you everywhere, which is why we are offering the eBook in 3 formats for only $10 if you have already purchased the print book.

Convenient and fully searchable, the PDF version enables you to easily find and copy code—or perform examples by quickly toggling between instructions and applications. The MOBI format is ideal for your Kindle, while the ePUB can be utilized on a variety of mobile devices.

Go to www.apress.com/promo/tendollars to purchase your companion eBook.